You Are How You Lead

YOU ARE HOW YOU LEAD

Deliberate leadership
on purpose with intention

RITA CINCOTTA

Published by Rita Cincotta

First published in 2023 in Melbourne, Australia

Copyright © Rita Cincotta

www.ritacincotta.com

Edited by Jenny Magee

Typeset and by BookPOD

ISBN: 978-0-6452963-2-7
ISBN: 978-0-6452963-3-4

 A catalogue record for this book is available from the National Library of Australia

To my Dad, Domenico Cincotta.

He was my coach and a leader who was deliberate and lived with intention and purpose. Dad had an abundance of authenticity because he knew who he was and led with that.

Rest easy, Dad. x

Contents

CHAPTER 1

The Deliberate Leader 1

CHAPTER 2

What Makes A Deliberate Leader 27

CHAPTER 3

The Importance of Self-Awareness in Coaching 43

CHAPTER 4

Earning the Trust to Coach 63

CHAPTER 5

Connect to Lead 89

CHAPTER 6

Asking the Best Questions 105

CHAPTER 7

Calibrate to Lead 121

CHAPTER 8

Support with Intention 133

CHAPTER 9

The Deliberate Leader Attributes 145

CHAPTER 10

Developing a Deliberate Leadership Coaching Culture 175

Afterword 209

About the Author 212

Acknowledgements 214

References 217

CHAPTER 1

The Deliberate Leader

*'If your actions inspire others to
dream more, learn more, do more and
become more, you are a leader.'*
— John Quincy Adams

Did you deliberately choose to be a leader?

Many of us did not. Being a leader was something that happened rather than something we chose. In fact, many leaders are not deliberate leaders. They lead with hesitation, reservation, a lack of assuredness and fluctuating confidence. Their teams feel this, as do their colleagues, senior leaders and boards.

Deliberate leaders are clear about where they are going and where they are taking the organisation. They are intentional about the team they choose and what behaviours, skills and capabilities they need on the team. They are conscious that strategy informs everything they do, so they ensure the purpose is clear and understood.

This book is about deliberate leadership. It's about leading with intention because you are how you lead. You are measured by how you lead. Your success and the organisation's success are directly linked to how you lead. It is a choice that requires consistency and the payoffs can be huge! Being a deliberate leader offers you significant influence, a clearer vision, broader experience and greater empowerment. Imagine being able to amplify all these aspects of your leadership. What would it bring for you, your team and your organisation?

If you have picked up this book, you are likely exploring how to be a better leader. Perhaps your current leadership style is not working for you or your team. Maybe you are not getting the results you once did. Perhaps you are looking somewhat enviously at how other leaders motivate their teams. Or maybe you are quite happy with how you are leading and how your team is performing, but you are curious about how you could encourage a higher level of performance and connection in your team.

This book focuses on coaching as a deliberate leadership style.

Leaders who deliberately choose to coach and incorporate coaching in how they lead have far greater success. They achieve more, enjoy leading and build quality relationships that last longer. Leaders who don't invest time in building such a deliberate connection feel challenged by a lack of motivation and interest in their team and what they are there to do. They see their teams as vehicles for getting stuff done, producing limited results that are, at most, the bare minimum. The job gets done but with limited enjoyment, connection or growth.

Leaders who coach, invest in their teams, developing connections, asking questions, calibrating what they know and learn, and supporting without assuming. The investment is further enhanced when leaders are self-aware and focused on building and maintaining trust in their teams.

The best leaders I have followed and observed are deliberate about building connections with their teams. They know a successful team is a tight unit. They know what motivates each member because they spend time learning about their team. For this reason, it is often seen as too hard, too challenging and with a limited guarantee of success. The leader acknowledges that this investment of time creates stronger, higher-performing teams that enjoy sustainable success.

It is well known that employees leave managers rather than organisations. A lack of engagement, poor culture, mediocre results and toxic team dynamics can often be attributed to weak leadership. Teams that experience any of these negative attributes likely have a leader who is neither intentional nor deliberate about leadership. They may see leadership as something they need to do in addition to their technical expertise and experience. As it's not their main game, their teams suffer and their results reflect their lack of focus.

Successful teams that feel great to be a part of are not serendipitous. There is a deliberate and focused effort on team dynamics. This considers the team's purpose and goals, and who is on the team — their background and capability, what they offer, and the collective strengths and gaps. Led by the leader, it

When we coach,
we observe, listen,
reflect and consider
how to assist,
guide, develop
and enhance to
bring about the
best individual and
collective results.

is carefully considered and planned. The leader's sustained focus on these dynamics contributes to longer-lasting team success.

There are many ways to be deliberate about leadership and achieving success. With multiple styles and theories of leadership, it is worthwhile thinking about what best fits your personality and team.

Do you prefer blended leadership that depends on what the team needs? Imagine you are cooking dinner. You have a little taste as you cook and realise it needs something more. You add salt and have another taste. Still not right. You add pepper and taste again. Better, but it's still missing something, so you add a new ingredient — fresh herbs. You wait a few minutes, then taste once more. And now the dish is complete. The recipe did not tell you to add fresh herbs. You assessed and added what you felt was needed to bring out and balance the other flavours and create a great-tasting dish. A leader who only ever relies on a recipe or instructions on how to lead misses the benefit of being adaptable and in service of the team.

A coaching style provides a blend of different leadership styles. When we coach, we observe, listen, reflect and consider how to assist, guide, develop and enhance to bring about the best individual and collective results. We are tuned in to our organisations and purpose, the goals we must achieve, and our team members' capability and development needs. We are responsive, which helps us to adapt as the needs of the organisation and our teams change. Coaching has become a popular leadership style that achieves results, as you will learn in this book.

Why do Deliberate Leaders coach?

There has been a rise in the use of coaching as a useful leadership style over the last decade, as it has become popular with conventional executives.[1] A coaching leadership style focuses on support and guidance rather than instruction. It respects the knowledge that both leader and employee bring to the relationship and distributes the power balance more fairly.

Before we delve into why leading like a coach might be a useful strategy for you, let's look at coaching at work. This definition from Bozer and Jones sums up the context.

> 'Coaching is a one-to-one intervention between a (professional) coach and a client (the team member or coachee). The purpose of this intervention is to enhance the client's behavioural change through self-awareness and learning, and ultimately contribute to individual and organisational success.'[2]

The focus here is on individual *performance* and organisational success. The most successful coaching strategies focus on individual and organisational success. This two-sided investment ensures that all parties are committed to making the coaching worthwhile.

In professional development, a coach can help individuals become more aware of their strengths and identify areas that are getting in the way of better performance. Coaches work to uncover challenges and opportunities and determine the goals to help meet the gap. That doesn't mean they focus only on the gaps. There is more benefit in leveraging and further developing key strengths rather than focusing on gaps that can be difficult to change. Organisations leverage coaching to address concerns such as developing behavioural and leadership skills, managing talent, fostering innovation and seeking higher performance levels.

Coaching can be seen as a form of systematic feedback intervention to enhance professional skills, interpersonal awareness and personal effectiveness.[3] It can also be defined as a guided, structured and monitored improvement-focused process that aligns participants with desired performance levels for their current roles or responsibilities.[4]

As a coach, 'you're there to ask good questions and listen intently, offer compassion, explore an individual's vision and build a caring relationship.'[5]

The popularity of coaching

Coaching is firmly set in great leadership, from the corporate world to the sporting field. Organisations know that the power of coaching contributes to successful performance.

When we think about leading like a coach, it's worth considering Ted Lasso, the fictional coach in the popular television series of the same name.[6] The show revolves around an American football coach hired to coach a professional soccer team in England despite having no experience in the sport. Ted Lasso emphasises the importance of empathy and positivity in coaching. He believes in building genuine connections with his players and staff, understanding their strengths and weaknesses, and supporting them through challenges. By fostering a positive and supportive environment, Ted Lasso encourages his team to reach their full potential.

Whilst very entertaining and light-hearted, the series highlights the significance of strong leadership and effective team dynamics. Ted Lasso demonstrates the importance of creating a cohesive team by fostering trust, collaboration and communication. He values every team member's contribution and encourages them to work together towards a common goal. By encouraging his team to persevere through difficult times and setbacks, he teaches his players the value of resilience, the ability to bounce back from failures, and to keep pushing forward. His unwavering optimism and determination inspire his team to overcome challenges and strive for success. The series emphasises the role of emotional intelligence in coaching and performance. He recognises the importance of addressing emotional well-being and creating a supportive environment where players can express themselves openly.

This next section explores more traditional coaching contexts and how they relate to leadership.

Sport coaching

Phil Jackson was the head coach of the Chicago Bulls from 1989-1998. He ensured he knew each of his players as individuals. Jackson understood what motivated them and how best to leverage their abilities. Even though Jackson used different approaches for different players, he was still able to focus them on a shared vision: winning basketball championships. This led to six wins over a nine-year period.

There is much we can learn from sports coaching that can be applied in a business context. In their 2022 Harvard Business Review (HBR) article, George and Clayton cite an example of the transition from sports to corporate coach.[7] Bill Campbell commenced his career as coach of Columbia University's football team and later became famously known as the 'Coach of Silicon Valley'. He was a trusted adviser and executive coach to many entrepreneurs, such as Google co-founders Larry Page and Sergey Brin, Apple's Steve Jobs, Facebook's Sheryl Sandberg, Amazon's Jeff Bezos, and Twitter's Jack Dorsey. Campbell is quoted as saying, 'Your title makes you a manager; your people make you a leader.'

Notable sports teams and professionals across tennis, soccer, football (Australian Rules Football), netball, weightlifting and even car racing all have coaches. If we are not actively participating, we may be spectators observing the coach in action. The coach's role is equally scrutinised when the team or individual perform well and when they do not. You are likely most familiar with sports coaching through watching or playing, as it has been around for the longest time.

Sports and individual coaching (executive coaching, life coaching, business coaching) share similarities in principles and objectives. The aim is to enhance performance and achieve desired outcomes through goal setting, skill development, feedback and analysis, motivation and accountability, mental resilience and continuous improvement.

In sports coaching, the primary focus is on improving athletic performance. Coaches work closely with athletes to enhance their skills, physical abilities and mental focus to reach peak performance. They help athletes set clear and achievable goals, break them down into actionable steps, and provide ongoing guidance and support.

Sports coaches analyse and provide feedback on athletes' performance, identifying areas for improvement and suggesting strategies to optimise their capabilities. They also play a crucial role in motivating athletes, fostering mental resilience, and instilling a sense of accountability for their actions. In a team sport environment, the coach also considers team dynamics, including how the team operates, performs, reflects and supports each other.

Executive, life and business coaches assist in developing leadership skills, emotional intelligence, decision-making abilities, and strategic thinking. These coaches collaborate with their coachees to set meaningful goals aligned with their overall objectives and guide them to break those goals into actionable steps. Feedback and analysis are vital components of any coaching, as coaches assess their coachees' strengths and weaknesses, offering insights and perspectives to help refine their approach. Coaches also provide support, motivation and accountability to ensure leaders stay on track and take ownership of their progress.

Sports and executive coaching acknowledge the importance of mental resilience. Sports coaches help athletes build mental toughness, concentration, and stress management skills to perform under pressure. Executive coaches work with leaders to enhance resilience, self-confidence and the ability to navigate

Feedback and
analysis are vital
components of
any coaching, as
coaches assess their
coachees' strengths
and weaknesses,
offering insights and
perspectives to help
refine their approach.

high-stakes situations in the business world. All coaching disciplines embrace a growth mindset and emphasise continuous improvement. Coaches facilitate learning opportunities, identify areas for development, and guide individuals towards refining their skills and strategies over time.

While sports coaching primarily focuses on physical and mental performance in a competitive athletic context, other forms of coaching target professional development in a business environment. The principles and objectives shared between sports and other coaching contexts highlight their common ground and the value they bring to enhancing performance and achieving desired outcomes.

We can learn much from sports coaching, and those coaches can also gain from exposure to other types of coaching.

Business coaching

While studying at university, my first professional role was as an intern marketing assistant for a newly-launched company called Business Coaching Australia. My role was to get the business going by approaching local small to medium-sized businesses and encouraging them to work with a business coach.

It was the late 1990s, and while coaching was not completely novel, the company had very few competitors. It was a new idea for many business owners who had no clue about what a business coach was and how they could help them. Typically, these businesses relied on their accountants to coach them.

They were often well-meaning and usually limited to finance — a critical business area, but not the only one.

Selling business coaching was hard. So, as a young grad full of ideas and enthusiasm, and with a word from my managing director, Alan, we approached the Essendon Football Club in our home state of Victoria and asked their coach, Kevin Sheedy, to be the guest speaker at our launch event. We were determined to help local businesses understand how coaching could benefit their businesses. And what better way to do so than to invite a well-known football coach to address them? As coaching was so well understood in sports, we knew this would help people understand the parallels in business and how a coach could help businesses grow and develop.

The event was a great success! It led to some new clients, but not enough to sustain the business in the long term. I went on to do other things, as did my managing director Alan; however, over the following decades, business coaching has continued to snowball in popularity in Australia and other parts of the world. The global market size was valued at USD11.6 billion in 2019 and is projected to reach USD20.9 billion by 2030. The industry has experienced a compound annual growth rate of 5.5% from 2020 to 2027, with projected continued growth in future years.[8] There are now business coaches who coach business coaches, and this area looks to continue to increase.

Life coaching

In pre-pandemic times, life coaching was growing in popularity. Post-pandemic, this growth has been supercharged.[9] There seems to be life coaching for all aspects of life, from new parents to retirees and everything in between. Trouble with your finances? Here's a money coach. Need some more energy? There's a well-being coach for that. Trouble with teens? Here's a parenting coach. There are even coaches for relationship issues. These coaches are not counsellors or psychologists. They are coaches. A quick internet search can find a coach in just a few clicks. Why are there so many coaches? If you have expertise in an area and are a good communicator with loads of self-awareness, you can build a side hustle or even your primary business in coaching.

Executive coaching

In full disclosure, I provide services in the executive coaching category, so mocking any coach or coaching style would be doing myself a disservice.

My experience as an executive coach has been built on almost twenty-five years in human resources and more than a decade in executive leadership. My experience as a board director and a graduate of the Australian Institute of Company Directors has also provided expertise that I share with those I coach.

However, I acknowledge that there are some barriers to offering coaching services. Having run a coaching business for five years, I know that if you suck at being a coach, you won't be in the business for long.

Internationally accredited courses and certifications confer professional status, but will they make you a better coach? Perhaps. However, I also know that you can develop coaching expertise through other methods, such as developing your professional expertise, senior leadership and board exposure, having self-awareness, strong communication skills, asking thought-provoking questions and showing empathy.

Executive coaching has long been an acceptable and regularly used form of coaching. Often reserved for those at the most senior levels of the organisation, it is often used to complement other leadership development and to work on specific targeted issues that require a bespoke approach.

The impact is unknown until the coach and coachee begin working together. The hurdles that get in the way of outstanding performance are identified through discussions with the coachee and perhaps the board chair or CEO. A coaching plan may then be created, including specific goals, measures of success, strengths and challenges and timeframes to achieve the goals. The coach and coachee then work together — usually for three to six months. During this time, the plan is for the coachee to develop greater self-awareness and increase their capability, particularly in behavioural competencies that improve effectiveness.

As the coachee experiences growth and development, other stakeholders also start to experience a shift. This may show up in personality traits or, at the very least, create a level of awareness so the coachee is aware of the impact of their behaviour and knows how to moderate it to mitigate the impact. Personality traits that are not useful or impact others can be stubborn to shift. The purpose of coaching is not to change someone's personality. It is about increasing self-awareness. That means that even when the coachee is no longer working directly with the coach, they

The purpose
of coaching is
not to change
someone's
personality. It is
about increasing
self-awareness.

have developed a system to become aware of the impact of their behaviours and understand how to mitigate any effects.

Typically, coaching in an organisation occurs using internal or external coaches.

Internal coaches

Internal coaches support employee development, motivate employees and teams and help them to reach higher levels of performance. Employees often have a clear understanding of the organisational culture and strategic objectives. They may be a part of the people team (HR) and sometimes have qualifications in organisational behaviour or psychology. They may be formally trained and recognised through the International Coaches Federation (ICF).[10] They may have been selected for the role based on other attributes that make a great coach. Or they may be leaders with formal or informal coaching roles.

Chapter Ten explores organisations that implement coaches directly as a key leadership strategy. These organisations have incorporated internal leaders who coach as part of their role. This book is focused on internal coaches keen to build a better quality relationship for improved business results in their organisations.

External coaches

When an external coach is brought into an organisation, they are often primarily used for senior executives or those identified as high-potential talent.[11] They may (or may not) be formally accredited and are often called upon for their expertise in creating awareness in the coachee and helping them set and achieve performance-related goals. Unlike internal coaches, they may not have a deep knowledge of organisational culture or a clear view of the strategy and political environment.[12]

Why leaders need to lead deliberately

I've written this book to guide leaders to lead deliberately. Why do we need to? The way we work has changed. Leaders are tired, overworked and leading in uncharted waters. Leading remote and hybrid teams is now the norm rather than an exception. The circumstances that leaders used to rely upon to lead aren't the same. Workplace dynamics have changed. Teams are dispersed, our methods of communication and collaboration have substantially altered, and we are all trying desperately to remain engaged and connected. These changes have created the urgency to rethink how we lead.

In today's fast-paced and complex business environment, organisations need effective leadership practices that empower employees and drive success. Leaders are finding their role increasingly tricky to navigate. Challenges such as inflation, recessions, maintaining profitability, leaning into rather than running away from artificial intelligence, dealing with talent shortages, and managing the ongoing complexity of a flexible workforce are only some of the difficulties facing leaders today.[13]

Leaders tell me they struggle to find time to manage performance and have difficult conversations. They are afraid to manage performance for fear of the person leaving and then having to redistribute the work to other team members who are already overloaded. Many leaders struggle to keep people accountable for deliverables and motivate the team.

The balance between wanting to be part of the team while being the leader is complex. It is particularly so when they have been promoted from within the team, going from peer to leader. Managing up is frequently cited as difficult. When asked about this, leaders describe 'managing up' as managing stakeholder expectations while maintaining the confidence of senior leaders. Some leaders face a crisis of self-confidence as they question their capability and impact in their leadership role.[14] They find it impossible to rely on old leadership styles, as ways of working have changed.

The challenges

Leadership is an esteemed path — but not necessarily an easy one. Plenty of challenges accompany it, with some more easily overcome than others. And, just to increase the load, let's throw in a pandemic with its ongoing complexities and challenges impacting workforces across the globe.

Many leaders are overwhelmed and exhausted by constant change, new information and shifting directions. Between work and personal challenges, there isn't much left in the tank. But somehow, they pull it together to navigate these uncharted waters. There isn't a playbook, as it's all quite new.

The leaders I work with strongly desire authenticity, which is hard in the current climate. To build and maintain team spirit, they have had to work out new, meaningful ways to keep their teams engaged and connected.

The ability to innovate spontaneously has also been impacted. Conversations that lead to an idea are rare (unless scheduled), and the impromptu aspect is diminished. Leaders must find new ways to ignite ideas and spark conversations among their teams.

It's time to look differently at leadership

Traditional approaches to leadership and management centred on a command-and-control infused style. In autocratic leadership, the leader retains full control and decision-making power. They make decisions without seeking input or feedback from their team members. Leaders direct and subordinates follow without question. The word 'subordinate' says it all. This style can be effective in certain situations that require quick and decisive action but can also stifle creativity and limit employee engagement.

In transactional leadership, leaders operate under a carrot-and-stick system based on reward and punishment. While results-oriented, this style focuses on maintaining order and achieving targets rather than inspiring personal growth or development.

Some industries still rely upon autocratic and transactional leadership. At the same time, many more follow modern best practices, including consultation, empathy, care, mutual respect, and interpersonal skills that foster trust and focus on the ongoing development of the relationship.[15] This kind of leadership style is present globally in democratic leadership, transformational leadership and servant leadership. Some leaders lead the way they are led, while others choose a different approach *because* of how they are or were led.

Alongside other styles, the leader as coach is growing as a powerful and valuable approach to leadership.

Coaching as a leadership mode

This book focuses on leveraging coaching as a primary leadership mode.

You may have chosen a leadership path, or it may have chosen you. Some of us have leadership running through our veins. It's all we ever wanted to do. We love setting a vision and mobilising a team to achieve it. Some of us set out in our technical area of expertise, only to find a few years in that we are provided with opportunities to lead the work we used to do and manage a team, too.

Whether you chose the path or it chose you, you now find yourself in the leadership role. This book is designed to help you lead deliberately and adapt your leadership style to a new way of working and living. It equips you with coaching practices to incorporate into your leadership style. These help you lead your team more effectively and with greater impact.

Coaching as a leadership mode is a collaborative and developmental approach to leading and empowering individuals or teams. It involves guiding and supporting team members and colleagues to reach their full potential, fostering growth, and achieving goals and strategic objectives. Leaders who coach focus on facilitating learning, fostering self-awareness, and helping individuals develop their skills and capabilities.

Leading like a coach means coaching and mentoring team members. We take on the role of facilitators, asking thought-provoking questions, actively listening, and providing guidance and feedback. Rather than directing or controlling, leaders who coach empower their team members to take ownership of their growth and development. They create a safe and supportive environment where individuals feel encouraged to explore new ideas, take risks and learn from their experiences. This increases psychological safety for individuals and teams. These leaders help individuals identify their strengths and areas for improvement, set meaningful goals and define action plans to achieve their goals. They provide ongoing support, encouragement and accountability to ensure progress.

One of the key principles of leaders who coach is their focus on individual needs and aspirations, tailoring their approach to meet the unique requirements of each team member and recognising their strengths, weaknesses and personal goals. They establish trusting relationships built on open communication, respect and empathy.

My dear friend Sandy Ward was one of my original leaders at AXA Australia in the early 2000s. Even today, I am grateful to call Sandy one of my greatest mentors and coaches. She has the rare quality of bringing clarity to the messiest issues. What I appreciate most

One of the key principles of leaders who coach is their focus on individual needs and aspirations, tailoring their approach to meet the unique requirements of each team member and recognising their strengths, weaknesses and personal goals.

is her ability to ask questions without judgment. Sandy's genuine curiosity unlocks mindsets and thought patterns that get in the way of clarity. Over the years, I have consulted with Sandy on many issues. She gently unpicks the knot by exploring the issue, asking questions and providing a balanced view. Sandy always leaves me feeling strong and sure.

Leaders who coach emphasise continuous learning and development. They promote a growth mindset, encourage experimentation, and provide opportunities for learning and skill-building. They regularly offer resources, training, or mentorship to support their team members' professional growth.

Coaching as a leadership mode fosters employee engagement, motivation and job satisfaction. It promotes a sense of ownership, autonomy, and personal responsibility among team members. Leaders who coach create a learning, collaboration and innovation culture where individuals are encouraged to share ideas and contribute to the organisation's success.

Developing a deeper understanding of your team

If we use one primary mode to lead, we may not cater to the individual needs of team members. In leadership, one size doesn't fit all. People have different needs depending on their capabilities and what's happening within and outside of work.

Leadership modes should be flexible to meet the varying needs of our team. Sometimes, you need to be more directive and supportive when delegating and coaching. Ken Blanchard and

Paul Hersey identified these modes in the situational leadership model.[16] More than fifty years after its development, the simplicity and ease of application of this model have helped it stand the test of time.

The leader determines which style might be best suited to their team member based on the development stage of their employee.

If you drive a vehicle with a manual transmission, you know you have to pay attention to the sound of the engine before changing gear. I don't pretend to understand this well. As a teenager learning to drive, my very polite driving instructor suggested to my mother that I learn in a car with an automatic transmission. Suffice it to say that my gear transmissions were not smooth, and there was much stalling. I think the driving instructor was seriously concerned about the well-being of his car!

A few decades later, while I have never returned to driving a manual vehicle, I have become better attuned to paying attention to the 'sounds' of my team, enabling me to know when to 'change gears'. I now impart this principle regularly in my leadership development programs, encouraging leaders to listen to the sound of their team's engine. The benefit of this metaphor is that the leader must tune into their employees' needs rather than leading in one mode (or in this case driving in the same gear). It is more adaptive and places the employee at the centre of the best leadership style required for them.

Reflection questions

What are your thoughts about developing your coaching skills to complement your leadership style?

How do you see this helping your team?

If you have worked with a coach before, what did you enjoy most about the experience?

How would you describe your current leadership style?

How would others describe your leadership style?

How would you like to enhance your leadership style?

CHAPTER 2

What Makes A Deliberate Leader

'To me, leadership is about encouraging people. It's about stimulating them. It's about enabling them to achieve what they can achieve — and to do that with a purpose.'

— Christine Lagarde

Now more than ever, there is an opportunity for the coaching leadership mode to shine. When a leader adopts this style, trust, authenticity and connection grow between the leader and their team, individually and collectively; defensiveness, hierarchy and judgment decrease, promoting stronger team relationships.

When a leader takes on a coaching style, leadership looks different as it is more collaborative. You'll see from the model below that it is based on the inputs of connect and ask that drive the outcomes of calibration and support. Self-awareness and trust are at the heart of the model as they facilitate the inputs and outcomes.

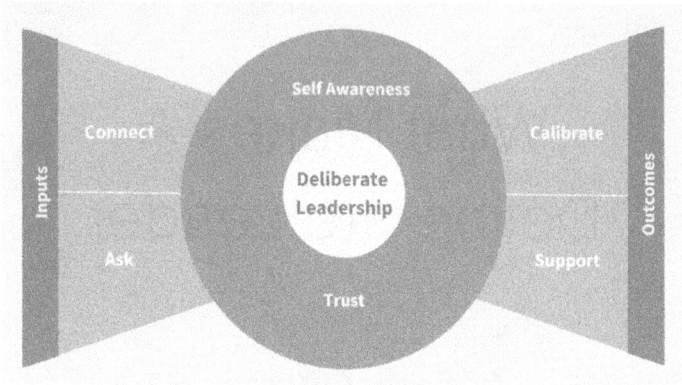

Figure 1: The deliberate leadership model

Let's unpack each of these dimensions.

The deliberate leadership model

Connect

The focus of the relationship is connection. When we connect deeply, we develop a deeper understanding of each other, our motivations and limitations, enabling the coach to better support the employee to improve performance. Empathy limits judgment and helps to view the situation from an alternative perspective.

Connection is essential in leadership because it builds trust, fosters collaboration and inspires others. When leaders establish genuine connections with their team members, it creates a positive and supportive work environment, promoting trust and open communication. Taking time to connect personally, listen actively and show genuine care and empathy creates a safe space for open communication. Team members feel comfortable sharing their thoughts, concerns and ideas, leading to better understanding and collaboration.

Employee engagement and motivation grow when leaders focus on establishing and maintaining connections with team members. It demonstrates that they value and respect them as individuals, meaning team members are more likely to be committed to their work, go the extra mile, and actively contribute to the team's success.

Support and empowerment allow leaders to understand their team members' strengths, weaknesses and aspirations. With this knowledge, they can provide personalised support, mentorship and guidance tailored to individual needs. Through connection, leaders can empower team members to develop their skills, take on new challenges, and grow personally and professionally.

Connection in leadership promotes team cohesion and collaboration and a sense of unity and teamwork. It strengthens the overall cohesion and collaboration within the team, leading to better communication, cooperation and synergy, ultimately enhancing team performance and productivity.

For one of my clients, Ashwana (not her real name), joining a new industry and leading a larger team came with fear and excitement. She was ready to leap into a more significant role but underestimated the need to connect fully with her new team. Self-assured and confident, Ashwana brought plenty of energy and ego.

In the past, she had built relationships based on her ability to get things done. However, she had also been in her last organisation for ten years. She had a reputation for being an executer with high energy. People knew her and what she was capable of. She joined the new organisation, leveraging her capabilities and intending to hit the ground running.

After a few weeks, Ashwana couldn't understand why people were not warming to her. She missed her previous organisation, particularly her team. Determined to replicate her success in a new place, she continued. Several more weeks went by with increasing disappointment and confusion, so Ashwana approached Tim (the friendliest person in her team) and asked for some insights. Tim was apprehensive about giving Ashwana feedback as he did not feel he knew her well enough. However, deciding that honesty would be best, Tim confirmed what Ashwana knew – the team struggled to connect with her. They felt she was all about results rather than getting to know them.

Ashwana was shocked but understood where this feedback was coming from. In an attempt to hit the ground running and demonstrate results, she had neglected to connect with her team. She had relied too much on getting to know people through the work — as she had done in her previous organisation. Here, however, they did not know her, and she could not rely on building connections through reputation. She had to be more deliberate in connecting with her team and other stakeholders in the business. Ashwana was grateful for Tim's feedback. Without it, she was unlikely to stay in her new organisation.

A focus on connection enables leaders to inspire and influence their team members. When leaders genuinely connect, they become role models and sources of inspiration. They effectively convey their vision, values and goals, rallying their team around a common purpose. Through connection, leaders can motivate and inspire their team members to achieve their best and strive for excellence.

Ask

Asking is a fundamental aspect of effective leadership as it is crucial in fostering communication, encouraging critical thinking, promoting engagement, and facilitating growth. By asking meaningful and thought-provoking questions, leaders can unlock valuable insights, empower their team members, and drive positive organisational change.

Asking questions promotes communication and understanding. When leaders ask open-ended questions, it encourages team members to share their perspectives, ideas and concerns. It creates a space for active listening and promotes dialogue, offering leaders a deeper understanding of their teams' and organisations' challenges, opportunities and dynamics.

Critical thinking and problem-solving skills are stimulated when we ask questions, leading to innovative ways to solve problems and creative solutions. Asking questions empowers team members and promotes engagement. When leaders ask for input and involve team members in decision-making, it fosters a sense of ownership and buy-in. It shows that their opinions and ideas matter, increasing engagement, motivation and commitment to the team's goals.

When I was relatively new to executive leadership roles, I experienced what it felt like to be asked questions that made me feel embarrassed, exposed and vulnerable. Sometimes, these questions came from colleagues and sometimes from senior leaders, including the board. It's amazing what you learn from painful experiences. We recall the hurt and quickly learn to avoid that feeling. These scenarios helped me develop how to influence and strengthen my preparation, but I would have preferred to learn from a more positive experience. Asking embarrassing or harmful questions doesn't create a learning opportunity; it simply causes pain.

Effective questioning also serves as a powerful tool for coaching and development. Leaders can ask questions that prompt self-reflection, encourage self-awareness, and help individuals uncover their strengths, areas for improvement and growth opportunities. Through targeted questioning, leaders can support their team members' professional growth, guide their learning journeys, and facilitate personal and career development.

Asking questions can spark innovation and creativity within teams. By posing thought-provoking questions that challenge the status quo, leaders can inspire their team members to explore new ideas, question existing processes, and generate fresh insights. This stimulates a culture of continuous improvement, fosters a learning mindset, and encourages experimentation and innovation.

When a leader asks questions, they become the learner rather than the knower. It takes vulnerability to ask questions more than answer them. I regularly invite leaders to consider the ratio of

When a leader asks
questions, they
become the learner
rather than the knower.
It takes vulnerability
to ask questions more
than answer them.

questions asked to questions answered. Could you challenge yourself to ask more than you answer?

Calibrate

Coaching requires leaders to synthesise information and identify the gaps first. The leader's ability to make sense of various data points is critical. Gaps can lead to unhelpful coaching direction, causing more issues than those addressed.

Asking and calibrating information are essential because they enable leaders to gather accurate and relevant data, make informed decisions, build credibility and foster trust within their teams and organisations.

Asking questions helps calibrate information by seeking multiple perspectives and gathering diverse viewpoints. Leaders can access a broader range of information by asking individuals for their insights, experiences and opinions. This provides a more comprehensive understanding of a situation, issue, or problem. Calibrating information through questioning allows leaders to make well-informed decisions based on a more complete and nuanced picture of the circumstances rather than relying upon judgments and first impressions.

Calibrating information also helps validate and verify the accuracy of data. By asking probing questions and seeking evidence or supporting facts, leaders can ensure that the information they receive is reliable, factual and relevant. This is particularly important in critical decision-making processes where inaccurate or incomplete information can lead to flawed conclusions and adverse outcomes.

Synthesising information through questioning demonstrates a commitment to thoroughness and accuracy. Leaders who actively seek to verify information and clarify any uncertainties build credibility within their teams and organisations. When team members see that their leader values accurate information and takes the time to validate data, it fosters trust and confidence in the decision-making process.

I learned the impact of not calibrating information when working with a team in the energy industry. My role was to help them connect better. The core issue we uncovered was a lack of trust. Team members described the leader as 'cherry picking' data points that supported their tightly held view on any issue. Over time, the team became less engaged and disinterested in participating in any activities involving problem-solving or innovation.

The opportunity for this leader was to become aware of their gap in calibrating information and to slow down so they could fully understand a situation before acting. Our sessions together highlighted this as an issue for the leader. Whilst it was a difficult message, the leader was receptive to the feedback and started demonstrating a slower, more considered approach in their decision-making. They found value in taking time to calibrate data before making a decision. This allowed time for more fulsome discussions as a team and a consultative approach.

Calibrating information through questioning helps identify biases, assumptions and potential blindspots. By asking probing questions that challenge preconceived notions, leaders can uncover hidden biases and potential gaps in understanding.

By asking probing questions that challenge preconceived notions, leaders can uncover hidden biases and potential gaps in understanding.

This promotes a more objective and well-rounded assessment of situations, enabling fair and unbiased decisions.

Moreover, calibrating information through questioning creates a culture of inquiry and continuous improvement. When leaders consistently encourage team members to ask questions, seek clarification, and challenge assumptions, it encourages a learning mindset and intellectual curiosity. This leads to a more dynamic and innovative environment where new ideas can emerge, and critical thinking is something the team embrace rather than something to be fearful of.

Support

Support in the coaching mode of leadership is contextual and subjective. It is not about what the leader can provide; it's what the person being coached needs. The coach's role is to serve. This is about listening attentively for whatever support they are requesting. If this is not forthcoming, the leader must ask rather than assume they know.

Providing support promotes employee engagement and job satisfaction. Leaders who show genuine care demonstrate that they value their team members as individuals. This sense of support and appreciation increases employee loyalty, commitment and motivation. Team members feel invested in their work and are more likely to go the extra mile to achieve organisational goals.

Supportive leadership also contributes to the development of individuals' skills and abilities. By offering guidance, mentorship and resources, leaders empower their team members to overcome challenges, develop new competencies, and reach their full potential. Supportive leaders create a learning environment that encourages growth, continuous improvement, and professional development.

Providing support helps individuals navigate through setbacks and obstacles. That doesn't mean the leader jumps in to act on the team's or individual's behalf. When team members face difficulties, leaders who offer guidance, encouragement and problem-solving assistance help them overcome hurdles and bounce back stronger. This support instils resilience and fosters a sense of confidence, leading to increased productivity and a positive mindset.

Supportive leadership also plays a critical role in fostering teamwork and collaboration. It encourages open communication, trust and cooperation among team members. When individuals feel supported by their leader and peers, they are more likely to share knowledge, ideas and expertise, leading to better problem-solving, innovation and synergy within the team.

A focus on support builds strong relationships based on trust and empathy. When leaders offer support, they demonstrate they are approachable, understanding, and willing to listen. This creates a sense of psychological safety and encourages individuals to seek guidance and share concerns. Strong relationships between leaders and team members facilitate effective communication, improve morale, and contribute to a positive work culture.

Self-awareness

When we choose to lead deliberately, there is no shortage of diagnostics, tests, quizzes, and formal and informal feedback mechanisms that can help us to become more self-aware.

Our opportunity is to know how to tune into ourselves to enhance self-awareness and calibrate this with what we know from others. Self-awareness allows us to adapt and respond in ways that best serve the situation and those we lead.

What we learn about ourselves as we increase our self-awareness may create initial discomfort. We may not like what we learn. It may not accord with the type of leader or person we think we are. However, part of self-awareness is using what we have.

My great-aunt Angelina is in her mid-eighties. She came to Australia from Lipari, a small island above Sicily in Italy. As a migrant, she has shared many stories of raising a young family with my late uncle Bob in a share house in Thornbury, in the northern suburbs of Melbourne.

At times, up to three families lived in that small house with a communal kitchen and bathroom, so my aunt learned to make do with what she had. As there were few opportunities to shop for food, Angelina had to be creative with what she had. While she now lives a far easier life, Angelina's ability to use what is at hand has been consistent. We have all loved and been amazed at what she creates.

Self-awareness is like my aunt's ability to leverage what we know and what we have. Our appreciation deepens, creating deeper trust in our abilities and what we can offer, and ultimately self-love. This is deliberate focus.

Trust

One of my favourite proverbs says, 'Trust arrives on foot and leaves on horseback'.

Trust is the foundation for every relationship. If you choose to be a deliberate leader, on purpose and with intention, you are also choosing to focus on trust. Once trust is established, building and maintaining it is not a given. It takes continued focus.

I have flourished when working with leaders when there has been high trust in our relationships. When trust was absent, the relationships were short and shallow. The same applies to teams I have led.

High trust is built deliberately rather than by chance. It's about credibility, reliability and connection. It means developing a deep interest in what the business does, understanding the strategy and goals, and applying and developing expertise to achieve them. We'll focus more on trust in Chapter Four.

What does coaching in leadership look like?

The following table identifies the differences between leading through management and coaching modes.

Leader as Manager	Leader as Coach
Focus on managing parts of the team	Focus on connecting the team, overarching purpose and goals
More answers than questions	More questions than answers
Judgmental	Supportive
Focus on weaknesses and areas for development	Focus on strengths and opportunities
Directive mode	Explore mode
Seek to resolve problems as they arise (whack-a-mole)	Step back to understand problems, then implement a strategy to resolve them
Seek to prove a point	Seek to understand
Solve problems through action	Solve problems by facilitating outcomes
Tend to be hierarchical	Tend to consult
Assert authority	Share accountability
Focus on team performance	Focus on team and individual performance
Decide what support the team needs	Ask the team what support they need

The Leader as Manager column reflects a command and control style of leadership. This style is dated and ineffective.

A more effective and commonly used leadership style is depicted on the right. It reflects leaders who coach. The style is consultative, open and inclusive. Leaders still make decisions; however, they do it more transparently, which is better understood by their team.

In the coaching style of leadership, the focus is on connecting, asking, calibrating and supporting. Self-awareness and trust enable relationships to be deeper and more effective. This promotes growth and development at an individual and organisational level.

Reflection questions

How do you currently connect with your colleagues? What has worked well for you? What would you like to enhance about your connection?

How often do you ask rather than tell?

What data points do you rely on when calibrating information to make a decision?

What type of support do you offer the most? How is this generally received?

How self-aware are you?

Do you find it easy or challenging to trust others?

To what extent are you already a leader who coaches?

CHAPTER 3

The Importance of Self-Awareness in Coaching

'You gain strength, courage and confidence by every experience in which you really stop to look fear in the face. You must do the thing you think you cannot do.'

— Eleanor Roosevelt

Tuned out or in?

If you think you've lost your ability to be attentive and tuned in, you haven't. Your attention has been stolen. This confronting statement comes from Johann Hari, the author of *Stolen Focus*.[1] He says the constant bombardment of messages, alerts, beeps, chimes, feeds, emails and other interruptions have shortened our attention spans as we deal with a never-ending stream of interruptions.

So, what has happened? Where has our attention gone? How does this impact our ability to be more tuned into ourselves? Is this encouraging behaviours, patterns and mindsets that keep us tuned out, creating a sense of disconnection from ourselves?

Tuned out doesn't necessarily mean we've hit the 'off' or 'do not disturb' button. In fact, it's quite the opposite — being tuned out limits our ability to be tuned in to ourselves. When we are tuned out, we look for external ports to tune into. We are focused on things outside ourselves. How are others behaving? What are they wearing? Where are they working? Who are they connected to? We devour a buffet of information, like sneaky voyeurs, peaking into lives that others openly have on display.

With a hyper-awareness of what is happening outside of us, we crave to know more and more about what is happening to others. While incessantly comparing ourselves to others may increase the burden of comparisons, it also limits our ability to have a deeper awareness of ourselves. We have reduced focus on our impact on others, our communication and our behaviours. With limited attention time, we have even less desire to look within, reflect, wonder or consider our approach for deeper impact. This has affected our ability to understand ourselves and others, demonstrate empathy and consider others' perspectives.

Knowing ourselves

Self-awareness is fundamental to emotional intelligence. The premise is that you need to know yourself well and be interested in continuing to observe, reflect and consider the impact of your behaviours, both positive and negative, on others. It's a subject that I'll keep addressing throughout the book.

But first, it's helpful to understand what self-awareness is really about.

To achieve maximum awareness, we benefit from engaging all our senses. This requires us to slow down and think intentionally about what we are sensing.

Beyond yourself, what are you aware of? Where are you right now as you read or listen to this book? Are you sitting in a chair, on a train or plane? Are you walking with my voice in your ears, listening and contemplating? What can you see, hear, smell, taste and touch? What's happening beyond you? Around you? Outside of you? Can you see blue sky? Can you hear birds? Can you hear a plane engine? Are there people talking, laughing, crying? Is there the smell of coffee, the ocean, food, or fresh rain? Can you taste anything? Are your hands touching the pages of this book, or are you feeling the softness of a blanket as you read or listen?

If you can tune into any of your senses, you are aware. You have a sense of awareness. You are tuned into yourself and what is happening around you. Perhaps you have noticed something in your environment. Maybe it has always been there, but you have not seen it before — not necessarily because it wasn't there but because you weren't aware of it. You hadn't paused to give yourself time to become aware.

Awareness, and particularly self-awareness, is a slow game. It's not very reactive. We have a greater opportunity to be more self-aware when we are slow and deliberate.

Surely, we are also aware when we aren't adopting intentional slowness? Yes and no. You can be aware when you are fast, but this is more reactive than aware. It is more about thinking and doing, rather than thinking, feeling and then doing. You are aware when you drive, but a good driver relies extensively on focus, thinking, anticipating and reacting. Awareness is in use, but it is a different level of awareness.

What is self-awareness?

In researching various definitions of self-awareness, I like this one from Greg Ashley and Roni Reiter-Palmon. 'Self-awareness is an inwardly focused evaluative process in which individuals make self/standard comparisons with the goal of better self-knowledge and improvement.'[2] Inward focus is about looking in and considering the outward impact of our behaviour. Self-comparison is about me against me, not me against someone else. I can look to others as a guide and an influence, but ultimately, it's me. I am comparing myself to myself. How did I react the last time this thing happened? What's worked well for me before? How will I now tune in to see what I need to do? What guiding principles will help me figure out how to deal with this thing I face? Just me, comparing myself to me.

Better self-knowledge and improvement are about a deeper understanding of self. Knowing how I react, respond and then behave. Making choices about the circumstances I expose myself to and understanding the consequences of those choices. Making choices that are better for me and limit the impact on others while leaving me in a positive mental state.

In short, self-awareness is about looking inwards, assessing self and improving to elevate leadership impact.

Self-awareness in leadership

In this book, my focus is on self-aware leaders who coach.

Why? I love working with leaders. I love supporting leaders who want to coach, by being more deliberate, present and connected. And I love leading.

As the first-born daughter of migrants, responsibility was thrust upon me from the moment I could make myself understood. Leadership is what I was born to do.

By the time I was eleven years old, I had a grand ambition — to become Australia's first female prime minister. The Honourable Julia Gillard stole that glory from me, and my aspirations for a political career (intentionally) never took off. However, my dedication to leadership has never waned. I had several leadership roles at school, culminating in my role as college captain (head prefect) at high school. By the age of twenty-four, I was leading teams at work, and I have not stopped since.

Twenty years later, I have led hundreds of people at executive level and as a non-executive director on a board. I love leadership and am grateful for the opportunities that have come my way.

If you have self-awareness, the constant spotlight of leadership is like a tonic. You cannot *not* grow. You are constantly adapting, evolving, responding, reacting, and planning for the circumstances you and those you lead find yourselves in. Yet it is not always comfortable to be under the spotlight. The searing light can get hot sometimes, impacting your decisions, how you make them, and their impact on others.

Growth can be uncomfortable, too. It can hurt. My kids have complained about growing pains over the years, and with valid reason. As we grow, things stretch. Bones and muscles move as the body's scaffolding accommodates expansion and movement.

We are constantly growing into our roles as leaders. Self-awareness allows us to understand better what we need to encourage new and consistent growth. What do we need to make it more comfortable, easier and enjoyable? Is it better communication? A focus on trust in our relationships? More attention to strategy and how to execute it? A better understanding of our leadership style? Whatever support is required, tuning in to what we need enables a better growth experience. It won't necessarily be painless, but we will be more aware.

Self-awareness supports leaders to coach

Self-awareness in leadership is about tuning in to know what sound you are making. My guitar needs to be manually tuned. Sometimes, I wish it would auto-tune (yes, I know I can get a device to help with this); however, I have only just started playing,

We are constantly growing into our roles as leaders. Self-awareness allows us to understand better what we need to encourage new and consistent growth and currently, 'playing' means one song. In the meantime, I am learning and loving it.

When I tune my guitar, I play each string and listen to the sound. I check that it sounds right; if it's out of tune, I tinker until I'm happy. Tuning in to my self-awareness is a bit like tuning my guitar. I pause often to assess, reflect and think about my next step. Then, I apply a new approach and learn something new. What next action can I take that will be better for myself and those around me? What will influence my decision?

Self-awareness is one of the competencies of a great coach.[3] It means they can understand the impact of their interactions on the person they are coaching. Without this, they are unlikely to work well with their team. If coaches are to raise self-awareness in others, they must be highly self-aware.[4]

In a study that looked at the role of self-awareness in coach development, researchers Carden, Passmore and Jones found that self-awareness requires readiness, willingness and curiosity to develop. They also found that self-awareness enabled coaches to understand their preferences, habits, behaviours, thoughts and feelings. This understanding gave the coach a different perspective on understanding themselves as an instrument of and for the coaching. It also deepened their understanding of their coaching identity, becoming aware of the impact of ego and relinquishing the focus of having to prove themselves.

Becoming hyper-self-aware can cause us to overthink. Observation and awareness without action don't provide the full benefits of self-awareness. To realise the benefits of self-awareness, we need to observe ourselves objectively, then come back into our bodies to act on those observations.

Awareness for action

Have you ever experienced a scenario where you realised a change in one variable could have led to a significant difference in the outcome? Typically referred to as a 'sliding doors' moment, thanks to the movie of the same name, we acknowledge that a scenario usually has multiple possible outcomes.[5]

In the moment between awareness and action, there is time, perhaps a moment or longer. Yet we forget about this space, filling it with worry, fear, doubt and anger rather than reflection and consideration. The coach's role is to remind you about the gap. This connects the person to their internal locus of control, which is their belief about how much they can influence the events and outcomes in their life.

Research suggests that awareness of the impact of emotions and knowing how to regulate them is important for leaders.[6] Learn how your emotions can affect you.

We also know that understanding how our brains react to certain situations can positively impact our ability to control a situation.[7] We may be unable to control our physiological response to a threatening or stressful situation, but awareness of what is happening can help us slow down and be proactive rather than reactive.

I developed the ARIA model (Figure 2) to encourage a deliberate pause before we act.

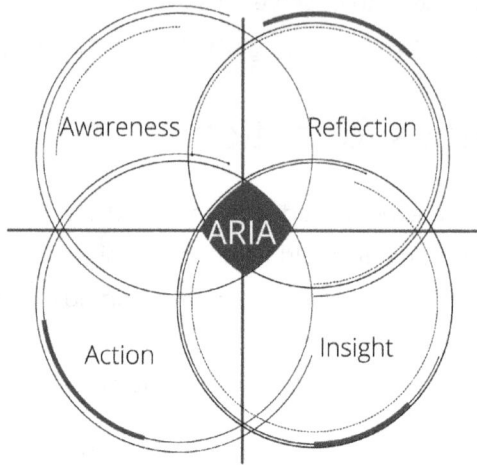

Figure 2: ARIA model

Steps in the ARIA model

In the first phase, we become *aware* of what is happening. We come out of our bodies and observe. No judgment. Just awareness. Here, we monitor our physiological and emotional reactions.

Next, we stop to *reflect*. We pause. We consider the situation. We do not react. How is the situation making us feel? What is the impact?

The third phase is where we develop *insights*. The pause has given us time to clear our heads and think more strategically, engaging the pre-frontal cortex of the brain. This may feel unnatural in a stressful situation, but not acting in that moment is worthwhile. Here, we reduce the confusion and create a clear path for quality thinking.

Finally, we move into *action*. We have had time to become aware of the situation and its impact. We have reflected and paused to gather our thoughts and develop insight before deciding to act.

Following this model avoids quick reactions and engages in proactive thinking. This helps keep emotions in check so they don't flood our ability to think. We are aware of our emotions and can be more mindful about how they are displayed to others, even whether we want to display them.

Emotions are a powerful internal alert system. We don't want to ignore them, and we don't want them to take over our ability to think clearly. We do want to use them positively and mindfully to feel confident in our ability.

When you are self-aware, particularly when you want to lead like a coach, you offer a more authentic experience for yourself and those around you. You get to be you. Fully self-expressed. Aware of your light and shadows. Conscious of which strengths to leverage and which weaknesses to mitigate so you can manage accordingly. We do it for ourselves, we do it for others, and we also do it for our organisations, families and communities.

Self-awareness is good for business

Leaders with greater self-awareness tend to get better outcomes than those with less.[8] Better outcomes mean improved bottom-line results. Higher performance, more innovation and creativity. Leaders who are self-aware and honest with their teams engender trust, creating better working relationships.

There are multiple
benefits for leaders
who understand their
strengths, weaknesses,
values and emotions,
and how these factors
affect their interactions
with others.

There are multiple benefits for leaders who understand their strengths, weaknesses, values and emotions, and how these factors affect their interactions with others. These benefits include:

- ▶ **Improved decision-making.** Self-aware leaders can better evaluate situations objectively, consider multiple perspectives, and make decisions that align with their values and goals.
- ▶ **Increased emotional intelligence.** Self-aware leaders can better manage their own emotions and respond appropriately to the emotions of others, which can help improve communication and teamwork.
- ▶ **Better conflict management.** Self-aware leaders can better understand the root causes of conflicts and find constructive solutions rather than getting caught up in emotions and personal biases.
- ▶ **Greater empathy.** Self-aware leaders are more able to understand and respond to the needs of their employees, which can improve motivation and job satisfaction.
- ▶ **Stronger relationships.** Self-aware leaders are better able to build trust and strong relationships with employees, partners and customers, which can lead to increased collaboration and business success.

Self-awareness is the foundational leadership skill of the 21st century, says organisational psychologist Tasha Eurich. She contends that leaders who know who they are and how others see them are more effective, confident, respected and promotable.[9]

It's worth noting that self-awareness is one of many important factors that contribute to deliberate leadership. Others include emotional intelligence, communication skills and a clear vision and strategy.

The importance of feedback

Research has long confirmed that high-performing managers have greater managerial self-awareness and are likely to be more in tune with assessing and rating their behaviours in the workplace.[10] Rating colleagues, including managers, in processes such as 360-degree reviews can be an arduous task. Alongside considering people's level of honesty or desire to sabotage questioning the validity of responses, we also have the results and debriefs to contend with. Some of that feedback can have a real sting.

I received some scathing 360 feedback in my first years as an executive-level leader. I was in tears as a very kind coach delivered it to me. The brutality of the comments came from my direct reports — my own team. Not my boss or my peers, but my team. I was devastated.

Their feedback didn't match my views. I thought I was doing ok, and my boss thought so too. I was achieving the plan, meeting her expectations and those of the board. I was 'managing up' well. However, my team members didn't agree. They felt I didn't consult enough. They said I made my points so strongly that they didn't feel they could offer a contrasting view.

The feedback process taught me that many of my issues were in my tone. I was too direct and too certain, so the team just went off and did rather than discuss and question.

As the leader, I had to be accountable; I couldn't blame my team. I was hugely disappointed that they hadn't given me the feedback before the formal review process. But I realised I had not built enough trust for them to feel they could. In hindsight, I doubt I would have listened, given my newness in my executive-level role. It's far more likely that I would have heard the feedback and become defensive.

In her book *Broken Open*, Elizabeth Lesser discusses how difficulty and adversity can literally feel like they are breaking us open.[11] It is the process of being broken down before being able to build back up. That's how I felt, yet that was when I really started to hear what the team was saying. I paid more attention to the formal feedback and how I was being received. I had open one-on-one discussions with my team where we discussed leadership styles, what they preferred, what was most effective and what I could offer.

We built trust. My willingness to listen rather than ignore them was extremely uncomfortable. I put myself out there at a time of immense vulnerability as I was the 'new kid on the block'. I was learning and doing concurrently, and had to make it look like I had everything under control — when the reality was far from it. So, I was brave. I continued to show up. It took every bit of energy I had, and in the end, it exhausted me.

My resentment grew, although only those closest to me saw it. I didn't feel myself. I was not authentic. I had not yet found a way to be me that also worked for others. I was acting like the leader they wanted, not the leader I was. I left that role after two years. The liberation I felt was unlike anything I had ever felt before. I was finally free. I was free to learn to be the leader I authentically was in a way that could work for others without compromising myself. I had woken up. I understood the feedback and made a conscious decision to act.

Without intending to make myself the hero of this story, I know that not all leaders act on the feedback they receive. Yet I knew that doing nothing was not an option. Not all leaders understand this; some simply continue their old ways. Whilst feedback is commonly referred to as a gift, I do not advocate acting on all the feedback you receive. You need a filtering process to consider the feedback and then determine what to do with it.

A filtering process for feedback

This filtering process is essentially a series of questions you apply to determine whether the feedback is useful and what you can do with it. Some example questions are:

- ▶ Why am I receiving this feedback?
- ▶ What is intended to occur once I receive the feedback?
- ▶ Do I agree with the feedback?
- ▶ Is the feedback fair?
- ▶ Do I trust the person providing me with the feedback?
- ▶ What can I do with this feedback?

- ▶ What would occur if I heard and applied the feedback?
- ▶ What would occur if I disregarded this feedback?

After I apply the feedback filter questions, I like to take the *gift* approach.

Treat feedback as a gift

Just as you can choose what you do with a gift, so it is with feedback.

If someone gives you something you love, you keep it. You cherish and use the gift, and it reminds you of them every time you use it. If you receive a gift you don't like, you could return it. Those gift receipts often provided with a gift are very handy. Another choice for a gift you don't like or won't use is re-gifting. That might sound ungrateful, but it provides a sustainable option, as the gift does not go to waste. And finally, if you really don't want the gift, you could just ignore it. Pop it in the cupboard, never to see the light of day, until you move house, or decide it's time to use it, regift it or just discard it.

Listening to everyone's feedback is like believing every bit of social media you read, hear or see. Some is useful, some is not, and some is just fake news. We calibrate what we read and collate information from various news sources. We decipher what to trust and know that if the news comes from multiple credible sources, it's more likely to be valid.

The Johari Window

Johari was a thing — long before Brangelina. (Google it!)

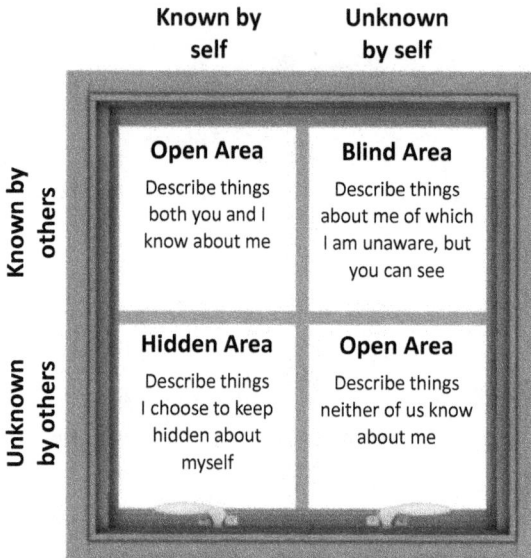

	Known by self	Unknown by self
Known by others	**Open Area** Describe things both you and I know about me	**Blind Area** Describe things about me of which I am unaware, but you can see
Unknown by others	**Hidden Area** Describe things I choose to keep hidden about myself	**Open Area** Describe things neither of us know about me

The Johari Window is a model used to understand and improve communication and self-awareness. It was developed by psychologists Joseph Luft and Harrington Ingham in 1955, who combined their first names to create the term 'Johari'.[12] The model consists of a four-quadrant window representing different aspects of an individual's personality and information.

Open area (Arena): This quadrant represents the information known to the individual and others. It includes behaviours, attitudes, feelings, skills and knowledge that are openly shared and understood by all parties involved. It represents the area of mutual understanding and effective communication.

Blind area (Blindspot): This quadrant represents information that others are aware of, but the individual is not. It includes blindspots, unconscious behaviours, or traits that others may observe but the individual may not recognise. Feedback from others is crucial in reducing the blind area and increasing self-awareness.

Hidden area (I): This quadrant represents information the individual is aware of but chooses not to disclose to others. It includes private thoughts, fears, insecurities and personal experiences that the person keeps hidden. This information is known only to the individual and is not shared openly.

Unknown area (Unknown): This quadrant represents information or potential capabilities unknown to the individual and others. It includes unconscious or undiscovered aspects of the person's personality, hidden talents, or unexplored potential. Through personal growth, self-discovery, and feedback from others, individuals can expand their known area and decrease the unknown area.

The goal of the Johari Window is to increase the open area, where there is mutual understanding and effective communication between individuals. This can be achieved through self-disclosure, receiving and providing feedback, and developing trust and openness in relationships. By expanding the open area and reducing the blind, hidden and unknown areas, individuals can enhance their self-awareness, improve relationships, and foster effective communication and collaboration.

I have recommended this tool to thousands of leaders, and I commend it to you. If you want to increase your self-awareness or encourage someone else to increase theirs, apply the principles of the Johari Window. This model increases self-awareness and trust between the feedback provider and recipient. It deepens the connection in the relationship and ensures that feedback continues to be exchanged.

Reflection questions

What are my strengths and weaknesses as a leader?

How do my emotions influence my leadership decisions?

How do others perceive me as a leader?

Do my values align with my leadership actions?

How do I handle failure and setbacks?

Am I open to learning and adapting as a leader?

CHAPTER 4

Earning the Trust to Coach

'Trust is the glue of life. It's the most essential ingredient in effective communication. It's the foundational principle that holds all relationships.'

— Stephen M.R. Covey

Have I earned the right to coach and lead?

Once we are on the path to self-awareness, the next step is to focus on trust and its importance in coaching and deliberate leadership.

Specifically, we look at:

▶ Trust and performance
▶ How to build trust as a coach
▶ What happens when trust is lost

Let's start by defining trust.

Trust can be defined as the willingness of an individual to be vulnerable to the actions of another party based on the assumption of predictably benevolent future behaviour.[1]

Think about five people in your world: a family member, a friend, a colleague, your leader and someone you don't know well but see regularly — maybe it's the person who makes your daily coffee or someone you see at the gym or on the bus.

How much do you trust these people? What do you trust them with? Can you think back to the moment you realised you trusted them?

If we go back to our definition of trust, we are willing to be completely vulnerable with these people based on our experience with them and the support they have provided.

The reality is that trust is built in micro-actions. It is didactic, meaning, in most cases, it needs to be two-way. It's hard to pinpoint exactly when you realise you trust someone. That is because it is unrealistic to recall every single micro-action. We likely remember the significant moments, but the micro-moments are harder to recall. However, they still contribute to whether we feel overall trust in the person.

Oxytocin and trust

From a neuroscience perspective, research supports that when organisations purposefully intend to build a culture of trust, this makes a significant difference in performance. American neuroscientist Paul Zak found that employees in high-trust organisations are more productive, have more energy at work, collaborate better with their colleagues, and stay with their employers longer than people working at low-trust companies. They also suffer less chronic stress and are happier with their lives, and these factors fuel stronger performance.[2]

Zak's research also looks at the hormonal impact of trust on our brains. Oxytocin is the hormone and neurotransmitter that plays a significant role in social bonding, trust and attachment. It is often called the 'love hormone' or 'cuddle hormone' because it promotes feelings of connection and trust in relationships. When released in the brain, oxytocin can influence social behaviour and enhance trust between individuals.[3] Trust is integral to every relationship, particularly at work. Trust between colleagues is vital for getting things done and how doing so makes us feel. That is, trust helps us achieve things, goals and targets, but if we are achieving and don't trust each other, our success will be short-lived.

Do we trust?

Does it feel like trust is wavering in society?

The Edelman Trust Barometer is one of the most comprehensive studies of trust, examining trust levels across various institutions, industries and countries. It is an annual global survey conducted by the communications firm Edelman. The report provides insights into the state of trust in society and its implications for four key institutions: government, business, NGOs and the media.

The barometer assesses trust across dimensions such as competence, ethics, transparency and reliability. The survey collects data from a large sample of respondents, including the general public, institutions and organisations.

The 2022 *Trust in the Workplace* report comprehensively reviewed how much we trust our leaders and organisations.[4] Across businesses, NGOs, governments and media, respondents had the most trust for business, with all other areas falling in their trust score. In the business category, the study looked at employers, coworkers, managers, heads of HR and CEOs. Many viewed their workplace as an essential source of community. That is not surprising given how much time we spend with our colleagues, physically and remotely.

The research also noted that we find it easier to debate issues with our co-workers than with neighbours. We seek societal impact through our jobs, perhaps because we feel that a grassroots approach to change could be more effective than trusting in government, media or NGOs. These societal changes include meaningful work that shapes society, opportunities to address social problems, power to influence specific business practices if employees object and a CEO that addresses controversial issues. The Edelman report provides four recommendations for employers looking to maintain and restore trust.

1. Trust your people: Actively seek out their views, act on their input and make transparent decisions.
2. Address societal issues: Do this even in the face of economic uncertainty. Connect people to societal issues through their work. Take meaningful action on climate change, fair wages, job training and inclusivity.

When you incorporate coaching in your leadership, you invariably influence the performance of the team and its members.

3. Bridge divides: Create an environment of mutual trust and civility and offer support for employees to do this via training and resources.

4. Restore societal trust from the workplace outwards: Publicly set the tone for civil discourse and encourage employees to become involved and participate with civility in their interactions outside of work.

The Edelman data shows that, given the existing high level of trust with employers, there continue to be excellent opportunities for leaders to build and maintain trust with their employees. If we want to be more deliberate leaders, we can capitalise on this trust and work to continue building and maintaining it.

Trust and performance

When you incorporate coaching in your leadership, you invariably influence the performance of the team and its members. This varies somewhat from other types of coaches, as a leader who coaches is more heavily invested in the outcomes of their coaching. If you succeed, they succeed.

Stephen M.R. Covey's book *Trust and Inspire* differentiates between leaders who lead by command and control, and those who trust and inspire. He says it is 'exciting and exhilarating to be lead, taught, coached, parented or helped by someone like this.'[5] Covey believes that a big part of why we feel differently is that these leaders think and behave differently. We perform better because of their interactions with us. They engage us rather than tell us, and they connect us to the overarching vision of whatever we are meant to be working towards. This applies equally to when we lead someone as their coach.

Trust has an impact on business performance. Paul Zak and his team ran an experiment that found those working in high-trust companies enjoyed their jobs 60% more, were 70% more aligned with their companies' purpose, and felt 66% closer to their colleagues. Compared with employees at low-trust organisations, those who felt higher levels of trust had 11% more empathy for their colleagues, referred to them by name 59% more often, and experienced 40% less burnout. They also felt a greater sense of accomplishment, by some 41%.[6]

If we want to use trust to help us drive higher performance, we can start by considering the role trust plays in high-performing and dysfunctional teams. In Patrick Lencioni's book, *The Five Dysfunctions of a Team*, the absence of trust is named as the first dysfunction of a low-performing team. The five dysfunctions model provides an excellent checklist for any team thinking about their performance.[7]

The dysfunctions model is also valuable for a leader who coaches. A coach wants to be able to analyse, review and improve team performance. If you start with the absence of trust, you can successfully work on the other dysfunctions. You can't skip this first one. The others cannot be addressed if this is not attended to first.

In a team that is dysfunctional or underperforming, the absence of trust looks like this:

▶ Hesitation to ask for help

We create trust within
and across teams
because it improves
performance. In
turn, this positively
impacts outcomes
for everyone.

- ▶ Team members hiding their weaknesses
- ▶ Avoiding each other
- ▶ Not sharing information that needs to be shared for the work to be done.

In a high-performing team, trust looks like this:

- ▶ A safe environment where people share their views
- ▶ Team members help each other
- ▶ Team members make time to spend with each other
- ▶ Information is freely shared for the benefit of the team.

We create trust within and across teams because it improves performance. In turn, this positively impacts outcomes for everyone.

The importance of psychological safety in building trust

Psychological safety is vital for a team to perform well. The term refers to an environment where team members feel safe to take risks, share their ideas, and express their thoughts and concerns without fear of judgment or retribution.

Project Aristotle was an internal research initiative launched by Google in 2012 to better understand and enhance team effectiveness within the organisation.

The research team at Google analysed vast amounts of data, including team performance evaluations, employee surveys and interview feedback, to uncover patterns and insights related to team dynamics. They examined a wide range of factors, such as team composition, individual skills, communication patterns and psychological safety.

One of the key findings was that teams with higher levels of psychological safety were more innovative, collaborative, and ultimately more successful.

The research also emphasised the significance of clear goals and roles within teams. When team members had a shared understanding of their objectives and responsibilities, they could better coordinate their efforts and achieve their goals.

Another insight from Project Aristotle was the role of communication and equal participation. Effective teams had members who actively listened to one another, showed empathy, and ensured everyone had an equal opportunity to contribute. Balanced participation and inclusive communication fostered a sense of belonging and enhanced overall team performance.

Project Aristotle highlighted the importance of soft skills, such as empathy, emotional intelligence, and social awareness, alongside technical expertise. It emphasised the need for teams to create a culture of trust, respect and support, where individuals feel valued and their contributions are recognised.

The findings of Project Aristotle have significantly impacted how Google and other organisations approach team dynamics and collaboration. The research has underscored the importance of psychological safety, clear goals, inclusive communication, and interpersonal skills in creating high-performing teams. It has influenced team-building strategies, leadership development and organisational culture initiatives, all aimed at improving team effectiveness and driving overall success.[8]

Psychological trust in coaching

Amy Edmondson is a professor of leadership and management at Harvard Business School. She writes, 'The academic research is overwhelming: when people believe they can speak up at work, the learning, innovation and performance of their organisation is greater. Teams and organisations where people believe their voices are welcome, outperform their counterparts.'[9]

Psychological trust is as important in a coaching relationship as in a team-based environment. Unless the leader who adopts a coaching mode does not intentionally work to build psychological trust, they won't create the right environment for leading and coaching across various challenges that arise.

In teams with psychological safety, there is comfort in making mistakes, as there is an appreciation that we learn from failure. Failure is embraced as we adapt and move on to the next iteration. Ideas are openly shared, developed, expanded and contracted until the team arrives where it needs to be. This leads to evolved innovation and decision-making as ideas have been appropriately debated and discussed, and everyone who needs to be involved has been included.

When psychological safety is missing

The obvious signs of a lack of psychological safety in a team are relatively easy to detect. These include:

- ▶ Belittling or insulting team members
- ▶ Ignoring or dismissing team members' opinions and contributions
- ▶ Blaming and shaming team members for making mistakes
- ▶ Gossiping or spreading rumours about team members
- ▶ Micromanaging or not allowing team members to make decisions or take risks
- ▶ Withholding information or feedback necessary for team members to succeed
- ▶ Failing to provide support or resources needed for team members to do their job effectively
- ▶ Bullying or harassing team members
- ▶ Discriminating against team members based on their race, gender, sexuality, religion or other identity factors
- ▶ Creating a culture of fear or intimidation where team members feel like they can't speak up or challenge the status quo.

Other signs are less obvious, although they happen more frequently.

- Calling on the same person or people to offer their view first
- Minimising value of contributions from quieter people in the team
- Not enabling enough time for an issue to be discussed/ debated constructively
- Over-reliance on humour directed at a few members of the team
- Breaking a promise/commitment
- Body language that conveys disinterest, boredom or other negativity. Lack of consideration about who is in the room, the meeting or the discussion
- Hypocrisy: placing inconsistent expectations on some and not others
- Leaders take credit for success when it should be attributed to the team
- Micromanaging and over-checking
- Heavy reliance on over-measuring and over-analysing.

Building psychological safety in a team

One team I coached faced a significant challenge. The board had confidence in the CEO to execute the new strategy, but they lacked confidence in the senior team, which created a conundrum for the CEO. Should they risk achieving the strategy while they develop their capability and try to gain the board's confidence? Or should the CEO swiftly make changes to the team to proceed with the new strategy?

The CEO gambled and decided to work with the current senior team.

Firstly, the CEO shared the board's sentiment with the whole team. Sensitive feedback was shared individually, and broader feedback was shared in team meetings. The team chose to see the situation as a challenge rather than a defeat. They were determined to build the board's confidence and execute the new strategy.

The team identified what was holding them back based on the feedback. Their communication needed work, along with their ability to work collaboratively. There were some trust gaps based on other projects not being achieved, and there was a lack of clarity on ownership of portfolio areas. There was also too much emphasis on the CEO doing most of the heavy lifting on communication.

To address these issues, they decided to champion open communication and actively encourage everyone to share ideas, questions and concerns. They established a no-blame culture in team meetings, valuing honesty over fault-finding. This approach fostered trust and allowed team members to admit mistakes, knowing they would be met with support and collaboration rather than criticism.

The team also practised active listening, genuinely understanding each other's perspectives, validating emotions and acknowledging contributions. This approach made every individual feel valued and heard.

Celebrating diversity was another cornerstone of their strategy. They recognised that different viewpoints enriched problem-solving and creativity. They embraced their varied backgrounds and experiences, actively seeking input from all team members. Constructive feedback focused on the work and behaviours so individuals could build self-awareness around their approach and adapt.

The CEO played a crucial role by setting an example. They openly admitted their mistakes and demonstrated vulnerability, creating an atmosphere where others felt safe to do the same.

This team executed their three strategies simultaneously, winning back the board's confidence. At the CEO appraisal discussion, the board chair commented on the CEO's risky but supportive approach.

This story provides some ideas on increasing trust and psychological safety in a team. Other options include leading by example, demonstrating openness, approachability and receptiveness to feedback. Establish clear expectations for behaviour and communication, emphasising the value of diverse perspectives and dissenting opinions. Encourage active listening and empathy, promoting understanding and respect for individual experiences. Foster constructive feedback, focusing on improvement and growth rather than criticism. Promote collaboration and teamwork with shared decision-making and problem-solving. Address conflicts promptly and respectfully and nurture a culture of continuous learning and improvement.

By consistently implementing these strategies, teams can foster psychological safety and enhance communication, leading to greater trust and higher performance.

Why trust matters in a coaching relationship

In a coaching relationship, a focus or goal is identified, and the coach and coachee work together to overcome the challenge or problem. Trust is crucial — without it, the coachee may be unwilling to be challenged by the coach. The coach may not be prepared to provoke or challenge the mindsets and views held by the coachee. Communication could be impacted if either person holds back from being open and expressive.

I like this definition from the company, Core Strengths. Trust in a coaching relationship is '... a belief in the reliability, competence, honesty, integrity, and positive intentions of your coach or coachee and the freedom to be real and vulnerable with your coach or coachee without being judged.'[10]

How to build trust as a coach

This section explores how you can build trust as a coach.

If you are a leader wondering whether your team trusts you, the research says you may well need to be concerned. In a 2023 global survey of more than 15,000 respondents, only 46% said they trust their manager to do what is right and only 32% trust senior leaders to do what is right.[11]

Trust is crucial
— without it, the
coachee may
be unwilling to
be challenged
by the coach.

These statistics are highly disconcerting given that trust is the basis of any relationship, including the employment relationship, and we know that employees perform better when they trust their leaders.

The trust triangle

In 2020, Frances Frei and Anne Morriss developed the Trust Triangle as they worked with Uber to get the company back on track.[12] Frei and Morriss say trust is built on three key components: logic, authenticity and empathy. (These apply to leaders who want to lead deliberately by incorporating coaching.) They believe that any time trust is lost or impacted, it can be traced back to one of three components.

Logic: I know you can do it; your reasoning and judgment are sound.

Authenticity: I experience the real you.

Empathy: I believe you care about me and my success.

Here's how this applies from the perspective of the coach (leader) and coachee (team member).

The Trust Triangle	Coach's perspective	Coachee's perspective
Logic: I know you can do it; your reasoning and judgment are sound.	I believe in your ability. Your idea has been explored and makes sense.	I trust your expertise because what you are asking or saying makes sense.
Authenticity: I experience the real you.	I can support you with your real issues and help you develop greater self-awareness. I appreciate the real you.	I can be myself. You create an environment where I don't feel judged or shamed. This enables me to be open with you.
Empathy: I believe you care about me and my success.	I commit to understanding your situation by being curious and seeking to understand your point of view without judgment.	I feel that you are interested in me and my success. It feels like you care when you ask questions and develop genuine understanding.

There may be times when the coach or coachee's perspective is not as positive as these examples. If this occurs, there is likely an issue with one, two or even all three of the trust triangle components. Even one component can impact trust, likely hurting the relationship. The slightest dint in trust makes it challenging to work with someone and communicate freely and openly with that person. If this occurs, it must be addressed.

Unlike a usual coach/coachee relationship, where you can more easily part ways, it is not as straightforward in an employment relationship. With so much at stake, there are even greater reasons to repair and rebuild the trust. Leaving it won't address it. In fact, it is likely to create an even greater trust gap.

The Trust Equation

Charles H. Green introduced the Trust Equation to explain the components contributing to building and maintaining trust in relationships.[13] The equation is expressed as follows:

Trust = (Credibility + Reliability + Intimacy) / Self-orientation

Let's break down each component:

Credibility refers to the perception of a person's expertise, competence and credibility in their field or area of work. It encompasses their knowledge, skills and track record of delivering on promises. Credibility is built through demonstrating expertise, being transparent about capabilities and limitations, and consistently delivering high-quality results.

Reliability is about being consistent, dependable and trustworthy in fulfilling commitments and obligations. It involves keeping promises, meeting deadlines and demonstrating a track record of reliability over time. Reliability builds trust by showing that a person can be counted on to follow through and deliver as promised.

Intimacy is the level of emotional connection, openness and vulnerability in a relationship. It involves creating a safe and supportive environment where individuals can freely share thoughts, feelings and concerns. Intimacy builds trust by fostering empathy, understanding and a sense of mutual care and respect.

Self-orientation describes the degree to which a person focuses on their own interests rather than the interests of others. It reflects whether an individual is primarily self-centred or genuinely interested in the well-being and success of others. A low self-orientation, where one prioritises the needs of others, fosters trust, while a high self-orientation can undermine trust.

The Trust Equation is useful as the focus on credibility, reliability and intimacy builds trust between the coach and the coachee. We are reminded that a high level of self-orientation acts as a trust detractor. Individuals and organisations can cultivate and maintain trust in their relationships by emphasising and enhancing these trust-building components.

Remember that
trust is built in
micro-actions
and that creating
and sustaining
psychological
safety is essential.

TRUST to build trust

Remember that trust is built in micro-actions and that creating and sustaining psychological safety is essential. TRUST is a simple mnemonic representing five things you can easily recall to build and maintain trust in your team and a coaching environment.

Time	Invest time in people.
	Make it quality uninterrupted time.
	Look for quality over quantity (shorter, regular one-on-ones are more effective than infrequent longer sessions).
Rapport	Inquire and care about the well-being of the person.
	Prioritise getting to know each other.
	Recognise and celebrate success.
Understanding	Listen and respond with empathy.
	Find out about their challenges.
	Help them to determine their opportunities.
Sense-making	Be curious about the context and environment they are in.
	Avoid judgments by engaging all your senses to understand their situation, including your intuition.
	Ask them more questions rather than assuming.
Tactical	Put the effort in, in understanding where they may be at.
	Share views lightly – enable them to get there in their own time.
	Ask them about what they need from you.

What happens when trust is broken

My usual opening coaching question is, 'So, what's been happening in your world?' In one conversation, the leader responded about a team member in whom they had lost trust. They told me of a situation that had occurred months earlier when the team member was still new. The person had disclosed private and sensitive information to their previous employer (a competitor), which found its way back to my client. This breach of trust meant a 'workaround' was created, so sensitive information was no longer shared with this team member.

That became the focus of our coaching session. We spent more than an hour addressing the breach of trust and the seemingly benign (but ineffective) workaround that had been implemented.

In this scenario, trust had been broken. My client had good reason not to trust the person, yet the workaround was hardly sustainable and further perpetuated the lack of trust. Sooner or later, the person would know they were not receiving all the information required to do their job. This would make them feel that trust was broken and only worsen a bad situation.

I asked the leader if they had provided feedback to the person they had lost trust in. They had not — they were waiting for the 'perfect moment'. They were concerned about the impact on the team, as the employee frequently and overtly exhibited frustration over particular issues.

As I listened to this through my coaching lens, many alarms sounded in my mind.

First, the person had only been with the team for six months. A significant breach of trust in such a short time is always concerning. Second, the leader was intimidated by the employee. Forget the power dynamics here for a moment; there are serious issues when anyone in the team is intimidated by another. My psychological safety warning alarm was certainly triggered. Finally, the leader's workaround of not sharing sensitive information that the person would need to do their job could, at some stage, lead to a more significant grievance against the employer.

Suffice to say, that our coaching session included role-playing the conversation. We discussed context and language as fundamental in enabling the leader's message to be heard and understood.

At the end of the session, I asked my usual closing question, 'Have you achieved what you wanted to from this coaching session?' The person replied, 'Absolutely and then some!' They were now equipped to have a difficult but necessary conversation. Trust could still be rebuilt, but it would need time, honesty, empathy, understanding and a demonstration from that point on of openness and transparency. The leader knew that trust could be rebuilt over time if they applied the TRUST principles.

Like a house renovation, much planning goes into maintaining trust. Next comes the building process, and then you sit in your house and enjoy it before (perhaps) embarking on further renovations. It is an evolutionary process that requires those in the 'house' (relationship) to constantly reassess their needs and what they are receiving. Is it still fit for purpose? What does it need more of? Less of? You don't want to be doing a major renovation all the time. Maintenance avoids the need for a renovation too soon after the last one.

Reflection questions

Am I transparent and authentic?

Do I listen actively?

Do I keep my commitments?

Am I approachable and empathetic?

Do I admit mistakes and learn from them?

Am I inclusive and respectful?

CHAPTER 5

Connect to Lead

'When people talk, listen completely.'

— Ernest Hemingway

Do you remember the last time you brought a new person into your team?

How did you connect with them? If you considered the process thoughtfully, there's a good chance the person is still in your team. If the connection was rushed, with little foundation to build upon, it probably created what I call a 'Jarlsberg cheese' scenario. Edible, but with a lot of holes.

When building a relationship with a team member, colleague or coachee, the higher the level of importance and priority we place on connection, the better the quality of the relationship. We can describe connection as the sense of well-being we feel from human interaction.[1]

In his famous and timeless Hierarchy of Needs model (Figure 3), Abraham Maslow established that people are motivated to achieve a particular need. When that is fulfilled, they move to the next one.[2] Represented as a triangle (although arguably not perfectly linear in attainment), the premise is that humans need to achieve the basics of shelter, safety and belonging before satisfying higher-level growth, such as esteem and self-actualisation.

SELF-ACTUALI-SATION
morality, creativity, spontaneity, acceptance, experience purpose, meaning and inner potential

SELF-ESTEEM
confidence, achievement, respect of others, the need to be a unique individual

LOVE AND BELONGING
friendship, family, intimacy, sense of connection

SAFETY AND SECURITY
health, employment, property, family and social ability

PHYSIOLOGICAL NEEDS
breathing, food, water, shelter, clothing, sleep

Figure 3: Maslow's Hierarchy of Needs

In subsequent years, Maslow's model has been expanded to include three other areas: cognitive needs (covering knowledge and meaning), aesthetic needs (which include appreciation for beauty and balance) and transcendence needs (helping others to achieve self-actualisation).[3]

When our sense of belonging is threatened, we can feel disconnected and lonely. At times we can desire this need more than our physiological needs. Belonging contributes to our feeling of safety and security. Leaders are responsible for promoting a sense of belonging in the team.

When we focus on connection, we strengthen relationships and improve performance. In a study of managers who coach, most believed that coaching led to positive outcomes, such as strengthening their connection with their team members and that their coachees demonstrated elevated performance.[4]

In this chapter, we'll explore the importance of connection in our role as leaders who choose to coach and how we can more effectively coach to connect.

We will unpack the coaching impact model and how we coach with empathy.

Coaching with impact

Many factors measure the success of the coaching connection, but they are largely subjective. Some organisations apply a return-on-investment equation, such as consideration of objectives, behaviours and relevance to overall business results.[5] This may be followed by calculating the impact of coaching. To what extent has coaching impacted the project, initiative or desired goals?

You could also consider a cost-benefit ratio. What has coaching provided by way of benefit and what did it cost? While this is complex and difficult to measure for each coaching relationship,

I understand and appreciate why some organisations would want to apply such rigour to calculating the benefit of what can be very expensive and time-consuming.

Measuring the impact of the coaching connection

If a leader is looking to measure the impact of the coaching connection in a less formulaic way, I suggest the following factors:

- ▶ Goal achievement
- ▶ Self-reflection and awareness
- ▶ Observable behaviour changes
- ▶ Feedback from the coachee
- ▶ Assessment of performance before and after coaching
- ▶ Engagement and satisfaction of the coachee
- ▶ Sustainability of coaching goals.

This list represents what we need to consider when measuring the impact of the connection between the coach and the coachee.

Evaluating the extent to which the coachee has achieved their coaching goals makes it possible to determine the impact of the coaching connection. This could involve examining specific outcomes, milestones, or performance improvements targeted during the coaching process.

The level of self-reflection and self-awareness exhibited by the coachee can indicate the effectiveness of the coaching connection. We can evaluate this through self-reporting assessments, interviews, or feedback gathered from colleagues.

The level of self-reflection and self-awareness exhibited by the coachee can indicate the effectiveness of the coaching connection.

These methods provide insights into the coachee's growth and development in these areas.

Observable behavioural changes in the coachee can also be measured through improvements in communication skills, decision-making, leadership style, or other relevant areas targeted during the coaching process. These can indicate the impact of the coaching connection and provide tangible evidence of the coaching relationship's effectiveness.

Feedback from the coachee is another important measure. The coachee's perception of the coaching connection and its impact on their personal and professional growth can provide qualitative evidence of the value derived from the coaching relationship. The coachee's engagement and satisfaction with the coaching experience is important.

Finally, evaluating the sustainability of the coachee's progress beyond the coaching engagement determines whether the coaching connection has facilitated lasting changes. If the coachee continues to demonstrate growth and improvement over time, it provides a broader perspective on the impact of the coaching relationship.

Another way to measure this is through the relationship between the impact on the individual being coached and the quality of the connection between the coach and coachee. Figure 4 illustrates this.

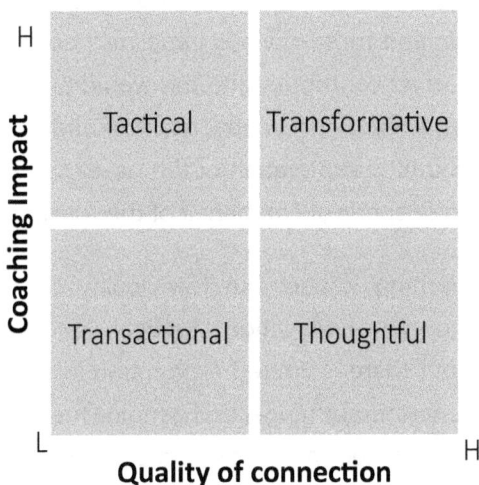

Figure 4: Coaching impact and quality of connection

Coaching impact refers to measurable and observable changes, growth and improvements in individuals or organisations attributable to the coaching process. It encompasses achieving goals, enhanced skills and performance, increased self-awareness, and sustainable positive changes in behaviour and mindset.

The quality of the coaching connection refers to the strength, depth and effectiveness of the relationship between the coach and coachee. It is characterised by trust, open communication, rapport, empathy, and the ability of the coach to create a safe and supportive environment that facilitates the coachee's growth and development.

When the coaching impact is low and the quality of the connection is low, the impact (at best) of the coaching connection is *transactional*. The coach and coachee meet and cover the basic and most obvious issues without much careful exploration. Factors contributing to this would be a lack of trust, self-awareness, limited connection, a lack of understanding and empathy, and limited exploration of the issues that may require more time and deeper work on behalf of the coach and coachee.

With high coaching impact but low-quality connection, the impact of the coaching connection is **tactical**. Coaching goals may be achieved, but there is limited exploration in self-awareness, sustainable behavioural change, and genuine feedback between the coach and coachee. A tactical approach that only looks at goal achievement could impact the long-lasting positive impacts of the connection beyond coaching.

When there is low coaching impact and a high-quality connection, the impact of the coaching connection is *thoughtful*. The coach and coachee are likely to demonstrate high self-awareness, empathy and understanding. They are likely to have a high level of engagement and satisfaction from the coaching; however, goal achievement may be low, and there is likely to be limited sustainability of the impact of coaching beyond the coaching.

Our ultimate position is to achieve a *transformative* coaching connection impact. Here, the coaching impact and the quality of the connection are both high. The coachee and coach are likely to experience all the factors described above. The transformative nature of the coaching impact means that the benefits are experienced long after the coaching.

Coaching with empathy

The ability to empathise in leadership and coaching has significant impacts on relationships and results. Empathy is about care, support, and understanding another person's perspective more profoundly. As executive coach Peter Bregman explains, 'empathy starts with curiosity'.[6] This frame is useful in using coaching as a leadership mode. Before we can feel and demonstrate empathy for another person's position, it is helpful to be curious, as this generates questions and keeps the mind open to learning. Empathy minimises judgments formed in first impressions and helps us to view the situation from one or more alternative perspectives.

Empathy is multifaceted. It is primarily about understanding and sharing others' feelings and perspectives. It involves putting yourself in someone else's shoes, experiencing their emotions, and demonstrating understanding and compassion towards their situation.[7] Empathy involves actively listening, showing genuine concern, and responding in a supportive and caring manner. It plays a crucial role in building relationships, fostering understanding, and promoting positive communication and connection with others.

Empathy in practice

In leadership, empathy is all that and more. It involves actively listening, demonstrating understanding, and providing support without judgment, allowing the coachee to feel heard, validated and understood. Empathy in coaching helps build trust,

Too often,
we confuse
empathy with
sympathy, pity
and compassion.

establishes a safe space for exploration, and promotes a deeper connection between the leader and their team member.

Too often, we confuse empathy with sympathy, pity and compassion.[8] Let me share a personal experience that helped me better understand empathy.

Our closest supermarket is at the end of our street. One day, I was out walking with my neighbour, and she needed to buy ingredients for dinner on the way home. As we approached the entrance to the supermarket, I saw a homeless person sitting in front of the store. They held a piece of torn cardboard that read, 'I need $38 for my accommodation tonight. Can you please spare some change for me?' I immediately remembered that I wasn't carrying any money and felt bad that I could not help them.

As we approached the entrance, my neighbour stopped and said hello to the person. She asked, 'Can I get you anything while I am in the supermarket?' The person smiled and said, 'Yes, that would be great. Thank you. Can I please have a banana and an orange juice?' 'Of course. I'll be right back.' We went into the supermarket; my neighbour brought her ingredients for dinner and the banana and orange juice. As we exited the supermarket, she handed them to the person and we had another brief conversation.

They told us they used to be a maintenance worker for a business that had shut down three years ago. Since that time, they had been unsuccessful in finding work. Their marriage dissolved, and their children, now adults, had moved away. After selling what was left from their post-divorce financial split, some poor investment decisions, and problems with drugs and gambling, they now found themselves living on the street, with the daily challenge of finding a place to sleep.

I learned a lot that day. I realised that even though I couldn't give money, which was their explicit request, I could help them feel a sense of belonging by having a conversation and listening to their story. Human-to-human connection. I also observed the power of asking a question to create a connection. My neighbour didn't assume what the person needed. How could she know? Not having been in that position, she could not presume to know what the person needed. She asked. Again, human-to-human connection.

I think the Potential Project nailed it when they described how to connect with empathy and lead with compassion.[9] They say that the two things that facilitate our move from pity and sympathy to empathy and compassion are our willingness to act to support and our understanding of the other's experience.

That day, as I read that person's sign, I felt pity. I had little willingness to act as I wasn't carrying any money. I did not know their story and had little understanding of their experience. My neighbour had empathy and compassion as she demonstrated a willingness to act. By instigating a conversation and asking what they needed, she gained an understanding of their situation. My feelings about this incident have moved, over time, from shame to opportunity. I felt shame that I did not have the same thoughts or actions as my neighbour. The opportunity, though, is that because of the experience, I have responded differently to subsequent situations. I learned a lot from my neighbour that day, and it has created a ripple effect in how I interact and respond to others I have met along my travels. At the heart of this learning is connection, brought about by empathy.

What is empathy in coaching?

When we demonstrate the willingness to support and are prepared to learn more about the person's circumstances and experience, we have the capacity for empathy and compassion.

Over the years, I have trained hundreds of leaders to become more empathetic. The method is practical and effective.

We start with an empathy map.

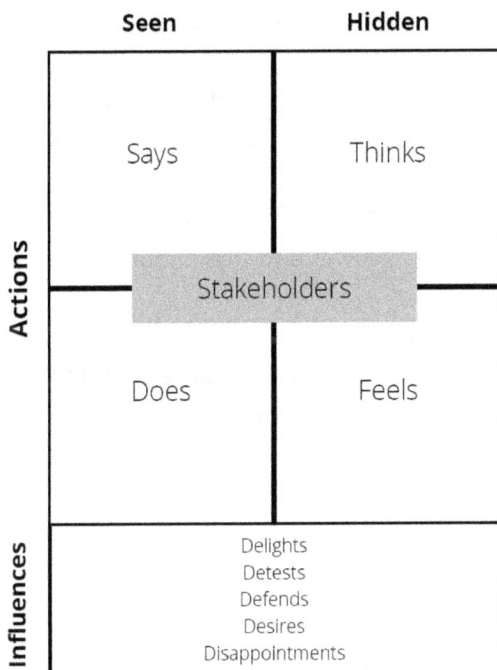

An empathy map is a tool to better understand a specific individual or user by capturing their thoughts, feelings, needs and behaviours. It is a visual representation that can help leaders develop empathy and create a shared understanding of the person they are coaching.

The map typically consists of four action quadrants: Think, Feel, Say and Do. Information is collected and organised in each area based on observations, experiences and interactions.

The *Think* quadrant explores the individual's internal thoughts, beliefs and emotions.

The *Feel* quadrant captures our perceptions of how they may feel about a particular issue we support them with.

We can't see the Think or Feel quadrants, so we make assumptions based on our knowledge and experience of the person.

The *Say* quadrant focuses on the external environment, including what the individual perceives and says about their situation.

The *Do* quadrant represents the individual's actions, behaviours and physical interactions. We can observe what the person says and does, so it is easier to capture these based on our experiences of them.

We can also capture what might influence the person. What delights them or disappoints them? What would they defend? What might they detest, and what might they desire? The influences help us to gain a broader perspective of their situation.

A leader can gain insights into the coachee's experiences, motivations and pain points by filling out an empathy map. This information can guide the creation of coaching goals and help develop a deeper sense of empathy for the person we are working with. The empathy map is a valuable tool to develop empathy, enhance communication, and encourage a human-centred approach to goal-setting, problem-solving and development.

Using the empathy map

As you complete the empathy map, you may find yourself in the Jarlsberg cheese situation again. That's ok. The holes or gaps in our empathy map guide us to ask questions and find out what we don't know about the person we are working with.

However, I always remind people not to bring the empathy map to the next meeting with the person they want to develop a greater level of empathy with. That would be creepy. Complete it before you get to know them, then work out where your gaps are. It will help determine the questions you should ask to create deeper empathy.

Reflection questions

How have my efforts to connect with my team positively impacted collaboration and productivity?

Is there a specific instance where I demonstrated empathy towards a team member's challenges? What was the outcome?

What strategies have I used to build rapport with individuals with different backgrounds or communication styles?

Have I encountered situations where my lack of empathy hindered effective communication? How can I work on improving this?

What have I learned about my team members' goals, aspirations and personal struggles through practising active listening and empathy?

How can I consistently integrate connection-building and empathy into my leadership style to create a more cohesive and motivated team?

CHAPTER 6

Asking the Best Questions

> *'The power of asking questions*
> *is the greatest power of all.'*
> — Swami Vivekananda

My friend George has collected questions for decades. Every time he hears a great question, he captures it. He has developed such consistency with this practice that he now does it without thinking. He has become unconsciously competent. This has been useful over the years we have worked together, as George always has the right question to ask.

When I asked George about this habit many years ago, he said it started when he began watching interviews. In the early part of his career, George watched movies for a living. (This is always a great line to open with at a networking event.) As part of his role for a large movie chain in Australia, George would watch new releases and decide with the team whether they would be played in the cinemas. He loved this job! He would also watch the accompanying press interviews supporting the movie launch, so he saw plenty of interviews.

Specifically, George was fascinated by the skill of English broadcaster and journalist Sir Michael Parkinson in asking questions that elicited the best response. George says there is real skill in asking a question, and I know he is right.

If you want to lead like a coach, asking questions will become your thing — if it's not already.

An effective question can unlock so much. Like a rock thrown into a pool, a great question can create ripples that leave the person thinking, exploring and reflecting long after your conversation.

This chapter examines why asking questions is so important in coaching and how you can always have the best question at the best time. Just like my friend George.

Telling versus inviting

Most leaders become good at telling, instructing and directing; it seems to come with the territory. It is certainly featured in command-and-control leadership, where the leader does exactly that. However, when we coach as we lead, we move more into the style of partnership and collaboration where we invite the person into a dialogue with questions.[1] That means less telling and more exploring.

Leaders often think they need to know all the answers. It's a myth about leadership. Great leadership is about creating the space for others to find the answers so they develop their skills and expertise. Doing so gives you a greater chance of creating trust, confidence and engagement in your team. How can this be done?

It's all in the types of questions you ask.

Open, exploratory questions create room for discussion and for people to express their views. If you believe that a leader needs to have all the answers, then asking more questions than you answer may initially feel foreign. It may leave you feeling weak and vulnerable and questioning your value. However, flipping this belief is essential to increase your leadership effectiveness.

Knower versus learner

We are more likely to be understood when our message and questions are clear. It can be hard to hear someone who is a knower. You've met them — the 'know-it-all' who always has a view and an opinion and asserts without inviting others to share theirs. They tell rather than invite. I have observed many over the years.

At the start, it's fine. They know their stuff; they contribute, appear enthused and are helpful. However, as time proceeds, know-it-alls tend to lose their shine. We tire of always hearing their voice first. Frustration rises as others have limited opportunities to jump into the conversation and share their views.

Avoiding being a know-it-all doesn't mean we have to know less. We must be prepared to learn more.

By asking more questions, you take on the role of the leader as the learner, as opposed to the leader as the knower.[2]

Taking on more of a learner than a knower mindset equalises the power dynamic between you and your team. It reinforces that everyone in the team can learn from each other rather than just from the leader.

Knower	Learner
Values knowing and defending reputation Does not recognise blindspots Defensive	Values being effective and learning more Acknowledges mistakes/ blindspots Open
Self-worth linked to 'being right' Hides doubts Argumentative	Self-worth linked to learning more Openly exposes doubts Curious
Definitive language States opinions as facts Uncomfortable in not knowing	Explorative language Owns their opinions Comfortable not knowing
Attached to thoughts and fights to defend the thought because it is seen as an extension of self	Not attached to thoughts and understands that thoughts come through them to be shared and discussed
Disagreements are personal attacks and a threat to self-worth	Disagreements are learning opportunities
Expertise + Certainty = Arrogance	Expertise + Curiosity = Humility

Taking on more of a learner than a knower mindset equalises the power dynamic between you and your team. It reinforces that everyone in the team can learn from each other rather than just from the leader. It helps everyone to feel increased value in their contribution.

Comfortable vulnerability

Asking questions helps clarify and genuinely seek to understand. It allows you to elicit information and get a clearer picture of the facts. In coaching, asking questions is critical. You can't rely on assumptions and judgments. By asking questions, you take on the role of leader as learner, rather than leader as knower.

Through asking, leaders pose more questions than they answer. It takes vulnerability to do this, and it can be a significant adjustment for a leader. If this challenges you, I invite you to consider a potential mindset shift.

Mindset one

Power is: When I know and I share, I am the authority. You ask, I tell.

Vulnerability is: When I don't know and I ask, I am the enquirer. I ask, you tell.

Mindset two

Power is: I seek to understand by asking thought-provoking questions.

Vulnerability is: Expecting myself to know everything when I may have gaps based on my assumptions.

Mindset one accords with how many of us were raised. Questions are bad because they make us appear inferior. In mindset two, we become aware of the power of asking questions. Knowledge increases through questions.

Leaders who coach hold the mindset that questions unlock while statements lock. Unlocking is vital, as we invite the person to explore, reflect, consider, evaluate and think. This promotes self-awareness and trust that the answers are already within them.

The foundations of the coaching process promote inquiry, challenge thinking patterns and create alternative ways of thinking, being and acting.[3]

Transformative coaching through great questions

In the last chapter, we looked at coaching impact and the quality of the connection. Ideally, we seek a transformative impact that sets significant and sustainable change for the person. That means that even though we may no longer be actively coaching them or in frequent contact, the self-awareness they have gained remains.

Can you recall a great question that resonated with you? It is memorable because you connected with the question and how it applied to you personally. When connection piques your interest, you attribute meaning to what you have taken from the question. When you connect meaning to the question, you draw a lesson for yourself. You might then share the question with others to 'pay forward' the feeling.

The significance of this process and the shift it creates becomes transformative. All sparked by a great question. Not a statement.

Not through someone else sharing their experience. The act of attributing meaning makes this experience memorable. It creates a real shift and unlocks what may have previously been inaccessible.

What types of questions should I ask?

Questions that stink of micromanagement are not used in coach mode. We all know those types of direct and closed questions.

'What have you missed here?'

'When will that task that is already ten days overdue be delivered?'

'I can spot what's gone wrong, can you?'

What you want to focus on are the big questions that promote exploration, insight and curiosity. These invite genuine collaboration and partnership. If you are a leader, you might be thinking about challenging or confronting questions that sometimes need to be asked about the details of the work. These can create dependency; they ask, you think, you answer. What we want is a scenario where they ask, you ask, they think, they answer. This creates less dependence in the longer term.

Before we go to a list of questions, let's consider our intentions. Every resource about incorporating coaching into your leadership discusses the power of great questions. But, to my mind, having the right question ready is the *second* thing to think about. The *first* thing is to understand the intention of the question.

What sits behind your question? What do you want to know? What feeling do you want to invoke? What do you want the person to do after they have heard and understood your question?

Question intention

What sits behind your question? What do you want to know? What feeling do you want to invoke? What do you want the person to do after they have heard and understood your question?

That's a lot to consider on top of a question that will unlock some answers. I'm here to make it easier for you.

When asked a question, I think about why the person has asked that particular question before answering.

This little pearl of wisdom was prompted by a leader I knew many years ago. When we reflected or debriefed a challenging conversation, they always encouraged me to consider the intent behind a particular question. My curiosity about why they asked the question helped me explore their reasons, motives and desired outcomes — and mine, too. Fundamentally, it helped influence and align views in a conversation. I was trained to spot the intent behind a question and have found it invaluable along my travels. That means I see how it can be applied when intentions that precede a question.

This focus on intent has also been useful in helping me to form the best question possible in a scenario.

The Question Intentions wheel (Figure 5) has eight different intentions to consider. Create your own list if you prefer; however, these are a good starting point.

Intent or intention is about the purpose, motivation, or objective behind a person's actions or decisions. It reflects the conscious or subconscious aim or desired outcome that drives their behaviour. In coaching, we can use our question intention to help us influence others' behaviour or thought processes. This next section explores the eight intentions and offers some complementary questions.

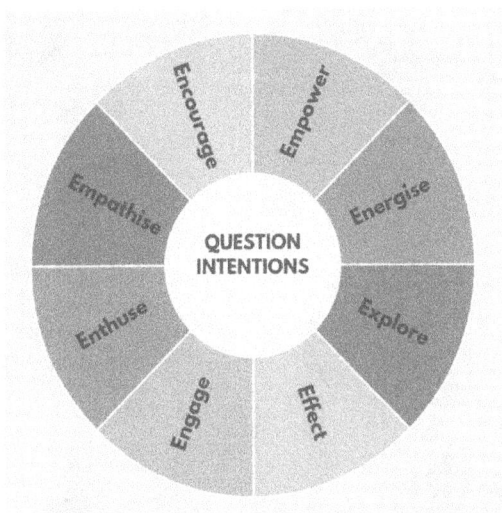

Figure 5: Questions intentions wheel

If your intention is to...	Some questions to lead with this intention
Encourage	What strengths can you leverage in this situation? What has worked for you in a similar situation?
Empower	What do you recommend would be the right way to progress? How do you envision making a positive impact or contribution in this situation?

As a deliberate leader, your primary role is to lead your team to deliver your organisation's vision, strategy and goals.

If your intention is to...	Some questions to lead with this intention
Energise	What is the most important first step you can take?
	What are you considering as part of your plan?
Explore	What else could be important here?
	What is the real challenge here for you?
Effect	What could be done differently here?
	What outcome are you looking for?
Engage	How can we make this conversation most useful for you?
	How can I best support you?
Enthuse	What inspires you?
	What's the best-case scenario?
Empathise	How are you feeling?
	What has been on your mind?

Considering the intention behind the questions means you can better lead the person to unlock the answer. Your conversation and dialogue contribute to their answer, but it should enhance, not overtake — just like adding a herb or spice to your favourite dish. You may really love cumin, but too much could overwhelm the dish and mask the other flavours. Questions should serve to enhance thinking, not overpower it.

As a deliberate leader, your primary role is to lead your team to deliver your organisation's vision, strategy and goals. Your role is to observe behaviour, tune in to what might be getting in the way of achieving these goals and help remove barriers and blockages. You won't always know what is causing these impediments.

However, learner mindsets will support you and the team to work through issues together.

What types of questions should I ask?

In her book *Multipliers*, Liz Wiseman talks about taking the extreme questions challenge.[4] She was tired of directing orders at home at the end of the day. Her colleague Brian posed a challenge that had worked for him. He suggested that she should ask questions of her children rather than direct them. This sounded ludicrous, and Liz imagined how it could potentially play out. However, given her level of frustration, she was prepared to give it a go.

That evening, rather than saying, 'Time for bed', Liz asked, 'What time is it?' 'Bed time', her kids replied. 'What do we do to get ready for bed?' Liz asked. 'We brush our teeth and read a story', said one of her children. This continued for the next 45 minutes. All Liz did was ask questions rather than make statements to her children.

As the children prepared for bed, Liz felt calm and observed that the children were too. She kept her promise of no statements, just questions. Liz continued this for several nights and was astonished that the peace continued. Over time, she was more balanced in her statement-to-questions ratio, however, she was more thoughtful about questions and statements and found that this challenge positively disrupted the pattern of statements and orders she was used to providing.

Increasing your ratio of questions asked to questions answered

If you want to increase your ratio of questions asked and answered, try this Extreme Question Challenge. At first, your team may still seek direction or a statement from you, but over time, they will expect you to ask more questions. It's not about being annoying or avoiding answering their question. It's about opening up the dialogue and getting them thinking more broadly.

Could you increase your ratio of questions asked to questions answered?

You could start big, such as taking on the Extreme Question Challenge, or start smaller, giving yourself a target of two or three questions asked with each of your team members in each meeting.

The aim here is to understand that your role as a deliberate leader is to unlock answers the other person may already know. Your key to this is to think about the questions you ask.

Reflection questions

What is my most valuable insight about the impact of asking effective questions on communication and problem-solving?

Is there a particular situation where asking a well-thought-out question led to a breakthrough or a deeper understanding?

How can my questioning techniques evolve after learning about different types of questions?

When did assumptions or biases influence the questions I asked? How can I mitigate these biases in the future?

How have I applied the skill of active listening in conjunction with asking strategic questions to facilitate more meaningful conversations?

How could I consistently incorporate the art of asking effective questions to enhance my problem-solving abilities and connect more deeply with others?

CHAPTER 7

Calibrate to Lead

*'Great leaders are almost always
great simplifiers, who can cut through
argument, debate and doubt to offer a
solution everybody can understand.'*
— General Colin Powell, former US secretary of state

What do you rely upon to know something? Is it signals, observation, data, evidence or intuition?

While knowing something may seem obvious, at times, it may not be as apparent as we think. How do we know that we know something?

When you lead as a coach, knowing stuff is important. You have knowledge and experience in an area that makes you the right leader and coach for your team and organisation. However, we can't rely on what we think we know. As explored in the last chapter, knowing or thinking that we know something can interfere with our ability to ask questions and be willing to learn, thus impacting our ability to lead.

Calibration to support our knowing

A great coach knows not to rely on what they think they know. Instead, they are constantly paying attention to data inputs. Assessing what they are hearing, seeing and observing through the interaction with the person they are coaching. They then measure this against what they know based on earlier calibrations.

To calibrate is to look for the gaps and realign. It means to carefully assess, set or adjust something, so we can synthesise and adapt to provide the best support.[1]

In helping understand human behaviour, the term calibrate is used in neuro-linguistic programming (NLP), where the practitioner brings together a variety of inputs that help them make sense of the situation.[2] Calibrating refers to the 'process of attuning oneself to the non-verbal signals that indicate a particular state in the other person'.[3] For leaders, the skill of calibrating is an important one. They have to synthesise information, make sense of the information they have, and identify the gaps. When leaders do this through the coaching mode, they are more carefully tuning in to create a fuller picture to help them best guide their team member.

Notice, observe, calibrate

We constantly assess and adjust our environment in response to our needs. Think about your day. You are continually responding to your energy levels and biological needs. If we think we are hungry, we source food and eat. But what if we are not hungry, just bored instead? Our bodies need to decipher the true feeling.

If we are unaware, we may mindlessly eat even when we are not hungry. We stop working at our computers, stand up, walk to the kitchen area and open the fridge. Are we hungry, bored, needing a leg stretch or a break from staring at a screen?

If you are self-aware, it's worth tuning in to determine what you need. Notice how you are feeling. Hungry? How long since you ate? It's lunchtime, and you ate breakfast but didn't have morning tea. Yes, it's hunger. Or is it 1.30pm and you've just had lunch but are back at the fridge? When did you last eat? One hour ago. Is it hunger? No. You just needed a leg stretch.

In both examples, your observations provided more data to help you answer the question of whether or not you are hungry. You calibrated these data points and determined your answer. In these examples, ignoring the signals could have led to a decision that would not have satisfied your needs. It is hard to focus if you don't eat when you are hungry, as blood sugar levels fluctuate. If you eat because you are bored, you will likely still be bored even after some food — unless what you ate was really interesting!

We need to follow the same process to coach effectively and lead deliberately.

Calibrating in coaching

In the example above, we looked at different data points in determining whether we are hungry or bored. When we lead as a coach, we also rely on data points. We consider factors such as:

▶ Communication: what we are hearing and saying

▶ Body language

- ▶ Mood
- ▶ Behaviours
- ▶ Motivators and demotivators
- ▶ Performance: is it occurring where it is expected to be?
- ▶ Capability development.

Communication is what we hear and say

Effective communication in coaching is the foundation for building solid relationships and connections. Leaders who coach must pay attention to what they hear and say to establish trust, clarity, and rapport with their coachees. By actively listening and asking insightful questions, coaches can deeply understand their coachee's needs, goals and challenges. Clear and concise communication allows coaches to convey instructions, strategies and feedback, ensuring that coachees understand and can implement them. Effective communication empowers coaches to guide and motivate coachees towards growth and enhanced performance.

Body language

What we say through our bodies can be more potent than words. Understanding body language is complex and requires significant analysis if we rely on body language to decipher meaning.[4] Over the years, I have agonised far more over words than what my hands were doing when I was speaking.

Coaches must be attuned to nonverbal cues such as facial expressions, gestures, posture and eye contact. A coachee's body language can reveal their level of engagement, confidence or discomfort, helping the coach gauge their understanding and emotional state. Similarly, coaches can use their body language to convey empathy, attentiveness and encouragement. Maintaining an open posture, appropriate eye contact and nodding to show understanding or provide acknowledgement can establish a safe and supportive environment.

Mood

Moods convey a vast array of human emotions, and it can be challenging to decipher someone's state of mind. Fast-paced walking around the office can denote anger, frustration, excitement, energy or happiness. Which is it?

Paying attention to someone's mood allows coaches to understand and respond appropriately to their coachee's emotional states. Their mood can significantly impact their motivation, receptiveness to feedback, and overall well-being. By observing cues such as facial expressions, tone of voice and body language, coaches can gauge if their team member feels confident, frustrated, anxious or motivated. This awareness helps coaches tailor their coaching approach, providing the right amount of support, encouragement and empathy.

Behaviours

Noticing behaviours in coaching is essential for several reasons.

Firstly, behaviours provide valuable insights into someone's patterns, habits and tendencies. By observing how the person acts and reacts in different situations, coaches can gain a deeper understanding of their strengths, challenges and areas for development. This understanding enables coaches to tailor their coaching strategies and interventions accordingly. A leader who coaches has the benefit of consistently working with their team, so they can track and monitor changes in behaviours over time to assess what might be going on for the person and the effectiveness of coaching interventions.

This consistency also makes it easier to notice behaviours that enable the coach to provide timely and specific feedback. By observing and pointing out positive and negative behaviours, coaches can offer guidance, encouragement and constructive criticism to support growth and development. Paying attention to behaviours can also be useful in revealing underlying beliefs, attitudes and emotions. Certain behaviours may indicate limiting beliefs or self-sabotaging tendencies that could hinder progress. By identifying and addressing these behaviours, leaders can help their coachees overcome barriers and achieve their goals.

Motivators and demotivators

Noticing motivators and demotivators in coaching is crucial for understanding what drives and hinders people's motivation and engagement. Motivators inspire and energise, while demotivators dampen enthusiasm and hinder progress. Awareness of these means leaders can effectively support and guide people towards their goals and enhance motivation and commitment. By recognising what inspires and excites people, leaders can tailor their coaching strategies to align with those motivators. This might involve setting meaningful goals, highlighting the benefits and rewards of achieving those goals or creating a supportive and positive environment.

Certain behaviours may indicate limiting beliefs or self-sabotaging tendencies that could hinder progress. By identifying and addressing these behaviours, leaders can help their coachees overcome barriers and achieve their goals.

It's equally important to recognise demotivators. Leaders can help people overcome challenges and obstacles by identifying and addressing what dampens their motivation. That may include exploring and reframing limiting beliefs, providing encouragement and support or finding alternative approaches to overcome barriers.

Performance – is it where it is expected to be?

A shift in performance is a key signal that something is going very right or very wrong. Over the years, I have supported hundreds of leaders, and at the first sign of a performance issue, I have always asked the same question.

'Do you know of anything happening in the person's world that could impact their performance?'

I am regularly surprised at how many leaders look at me like I have just flicked on a light switch in their heads. Many never consider that what happens outside of work may contribute to a change in performance. Ironically, this should be one of the first places you look if you think something is not quite right for the person you are working with.

Daniel was increasingly frustrated with Gemma's performance (not their real names). Gemma was not a star but was a consistently solid performer. Daniel noticed that Gemma's attitude had shifted. She had been at the organisation for some time, but recently, she turned up late when she was in the office and tended to be offline quite a bit when working from home. Daniel tried dropping a few hints through sarcastic remarks about being late, but it still didn't shift the emerging pattern of apparent disengagement. All that Daniel had calibrated was what he could see. He didn't ask questions or investigate why Gemma appeared to be disengaged. He planned to raise the issues with Gemma at their next one-on-one.

I was coaching Daniel at the time and, thankfully, he mentioned this issue in one of our sessions. I thought Daniel was missing a significant piece of information. He had only calibrated what he knew or thought he knew rather than finding out what was happening for Gemma.

We worked through some questions that he could ask Gemma that would give him more insight. It tuned out that Gemma had some health issues that required her to take regular breaks. As she worked from home more than in the office, she thought she could manage without telling her team about it. Daniel built a deeper connection with Gemma by asking gentle questions that gave him a clearer picture of what was happening. He calibrated the information and was better able to understand and offer support. Gemma, her doctor and Daniel worked out a plan that enabled her to take the breaks she needed. Three months later, Gemma was in better health and resumed her previous work schedule.

Capability development

As a leader, I have always sought ways to develop my team members. When determining what would best fit their needs, we looked at leveraging strengths and closing gaps if they wanted to move ahead. Before giving them something new, I would work with them to look at what they already knew, what they needed to discover, and how they could do so. Assessing capability development is a constant calibration exercise. Does the person have the capability to do what you're asking them? If not, what do they need? How will they access this? In what timeframe? And repeat.

Calibrating the data points

We must rely on our ability to observe these factors as data points to avoid assumptions and judgments. If one of the team appears withdrawn and sad, we cannot know if their mood is due to work or a personal issue — unless we ask. Even then, there needs to be trust for them to be comfortable disclosing the issue. There needs to be a solid connection. In asking the question, the leader must be empathetic to their situation. You can't fully know what is happening, but your observations tell you something is up, so ask your question lightly and empathetically. Then, carefully calibrate what you know from all the data points. Coach based on observation rather than judgment and what you think you know.

Let's look at how calibrating works for a leader who coaches.

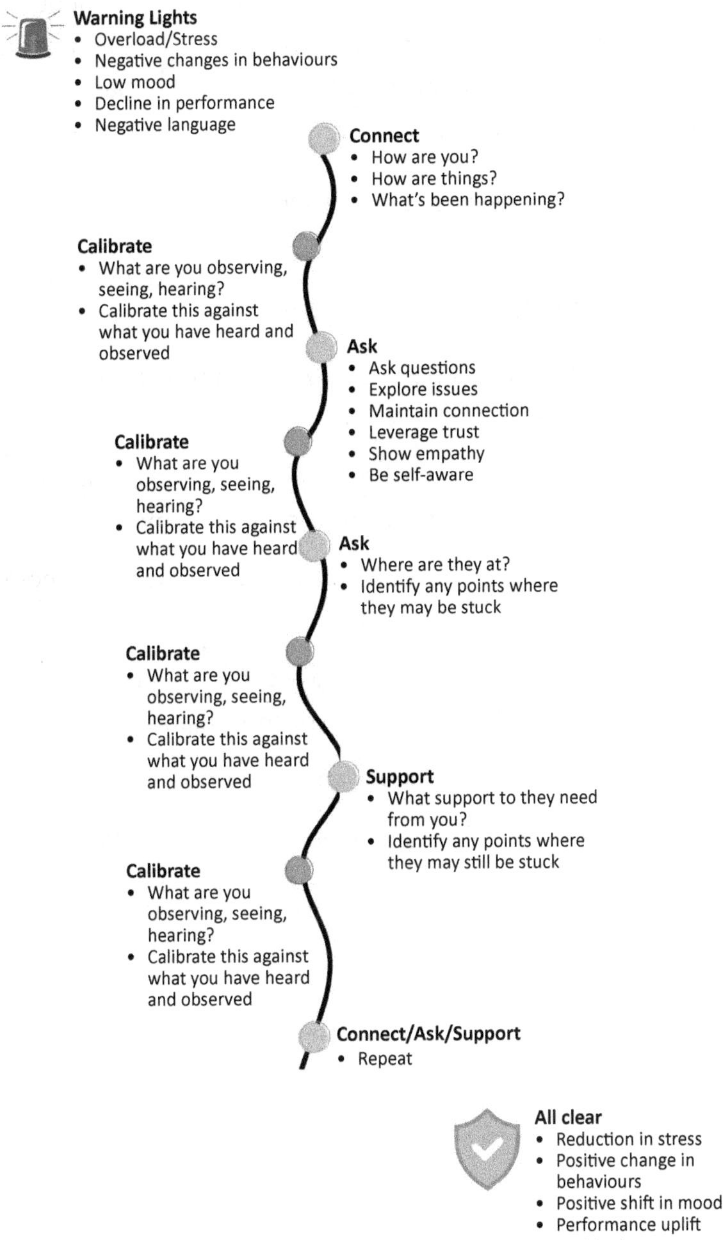

Warning Lights
- Overload/Stress
- Negative changes in behaviours
- Low mood
- Decline in performance
- Negative language

Connect
- How are you?
- How are things?
- What's been happening?

Calibrate
- What are you observing, seeing, hearing?
- Calibrate this against what you have heard and observed

Ask
- Ask questions
- Explore issues
- Maintain connection
- Leverage trust
- Show empathy
- Be self-aware

Calibrate
- What are you observing, seeing, hearing?
- Calibrate this against what you have heard and observed

Ask
- Where are they at?
- Identify any points where they may be stuck

Calibrate
- What are you observing, seeing, hearing?
- Calibrate this against what you have heard and observed

Support
- What support to they need from you?
- Identify any points where they may still be stuck

Calibrate
- What are you observing, seeing, hearing?
- Calibrate this against what you have heard and observed

Connect/Ask/Support
- Repeat

All clear
- Reduction in stress
- Positive change in behaviours
- Positive shift in mood
- Performance uplift
- Positive language

Figure 6: Calibration process

131

The process of calibration is ongoing and continuous. Pay attention to each data point so you are not relying on what you think you know but on what you observe based on your experience of this person.

We notice, observe and calibrate. On repeat. All day. Every day.

Reflection questions

What data points do I usually rely on to help me make decisions?

How observant am I of body language, mood, motivators and demotivators and how these impact communication?

How could I enhance my ability to communicate more effectively?

What prompts could I put in place that would remind me to calibrate when I connect, ask and support?

When faced with a performance issue, how do I respond?

How can I enhance my ability to work through a performance issue?

CHAPTER 8

Support with Intention

*'Leadership is an action,
not a position.'*
— Donald McGannon

Leaders have told me over many years that supporting their team while managing performance is challenging. For many, the two seem to conflict.

We may be overcomplicating providing support. We make it about us rather than how we can best support them.

If I only had one line to summarise this chapter, it would be in the form of a question.

'How can I best support you?'

If you have ever been in one of my leadership development programs, you probably remember me saying this is the most crucial question in your deliberate leader's toolkit. It's a big call, and I wholeheartedly believe it.

When we support someone, we are not doing something for them but supporting them to do something. It's like scaffolding. Builders build houses with scaffolding. The builders build, and the scaffolding holds them up so they can build. It's safe, sturdy, effective and serves its purpose.

Leaders who coach are like scaffolding. It's important to recognise the important role you play in scaffolding. If you try to build without providing support, the integrity of the building process is compromised.

'How can I best support you?' is the starting point in determining the support someone may need and the scaffolding you can provide.

Now, let's look at what can happen after you ask the question. There are three typical scenarios.

They articulate the support they need

They are clear and direct in what they need from you. All you have to do is work out how to provide the support. You may also need to decide whether you should provide the support. Is it scaffolding? Then, yes, it fits within your remit. Is it building? Then, no. Explore why they need that support and determine where else to get the support. Is it training, assistance from someone else or reviewing timeframes?

They say they don't need any support

This response is challenging when you can see what they may need. After calibrating all the data points (capability, behaviours,

When we support
someone, we are not
doing something for
them but supporting
them to do something.
It's like scaffolding.

motivation), if you agree they don't need any support, you could check in with them later (tomorrow or next week — it's up to you). If your calibration tells you they need support but don't want it from you, don't impose. This impacts trust and is disempowering. You could offer options if they feel they need support at a later stage. This could include you being available or suggesting they could work with someone else. Maybe someone else in the team? Remind them here that if anything changes, support is available for them.

They are unsure about what support they need or whether they need any

In some ways, the ambiguity here is challenging; however, if you follow the process for calibrating described in Chapter Seven, this ambiguity reduces as you rely on connection, exploration and observation. What are you noticing? What are you observing? And what perspective does calibrating these data points give you?

This is your way forward. If the person is unsure about what support they need, it is tempting to become the builder. You can see what needs to be done, and sure that it's quicker and easier if you jump in and do it. Don't be tempted to do this. It can feel completely disempowering and create a loss of trust and confidence if you jump in and the person feels inadequate. It can also be a missed development opportunity for the person. You want to teach them to fish, not fish for them.

What support looks like when we deliberately lead like a coach

Support is subjective. What I may interpret as supportive may feel the opposite to someone else. It's useful to think about what we want a person to feel and do due to our support. It's about tailoring. We want it to fit them well. When something fits well, we wear it; it's comfortable, and we feel good in it. We want support to feel like this for the person we work with.

Support in a leadership setting isn't necessarily about solving the problem. It is, however, about assessing what is required for the person. Some people need more hands-on support, which may involve providing direction and instructions, and removing barriers and blockages. For others, support may be about being a sounding board so they can bounce an idea but continue to navigate through the issue. The type of support a leader can provide in the coaching mode of leadership is entirely contextual and subjective. Leaders are encouraged to lean on the 'ask' mode to determine the best type of support for their team members.

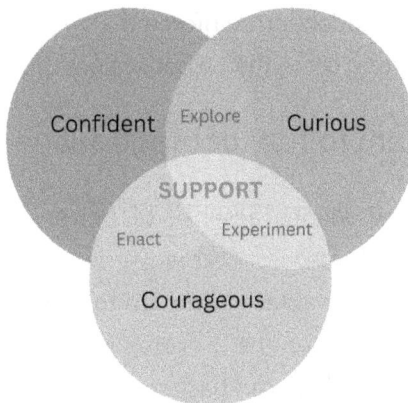

Figure 7: Coaching support

The support model in Figure 7 considers three things we want the person to feel and three things we want them to do. We add shades to these words to explore them in greater detail and create a bespoke support approach. I encourage you to do this so you can personalise their support.

We want them to feel confident

When someone needs support, confidence can take a hit. Feelings of inadequacy may creep in, especially if they don't like asking for help. Your trust and connection with this person should make them confident to seek your help. The support you provide should be empowering. The key is to remember that you are not building; they are. You provide the scaffolding, which frees them to learn and creates sustainability in your support.

We want them to feel curious

We are more likely to work out how to do a task when held accountable. It takes curiosity, a problem-solving mindset and a tolerance for risk. The approach may (or may not) work, but leaders can role model and reinforce that we learn more when we get things wrong more than when we get things right.

We want them to feel courageous

Courage is to experience a sense of bravery, resilience, and determination in the face of fear, adversity, or uncertainty. It is a state of mind that enables individuals to overcome challenges and take risks, even when the outcome is uncertain or the path ahead seems difficult. You can back someone to feel courageous — not by removing fear but by the willingness to confront and navigate it. That could involve encouraging them to step outside their comfort zone and embrace vulnerability and the possibility of failure.

We want them to explore

If the person we are coaching feels confident and curious, they are willing to explore. Their confidence complements their curiosity. Like a maze, there will be paths to try — some successful and some not. There is learning in exploration. We don't tell them what we know but support them to explore through questions, building their understanding of what they know.

We want them to experiment

If your team member is curious and courageous, they are more willing to experiment. You want them to experiment with what they have explored. That means they may look for support in taking a risk, making a decision and maybe even trying something that takes them out of their comfort zone. The best support you can provide is through questions. Ask what they are thinking and what they might do next. What would make this next move possible? What do they feel they need to experiment with? Stretch their thinking and encourage them to consider something different.

We want them to enact

Enact is at the intersection of confident and courageous. Here, we want them to act on what they discovered through exploration and experimentation. The only support required may be encouragement. It could be about empowering them to 'go for it'. It's not about telling them to 'fake it until they make it'. We can support someone to enact something by asking what they might need. Where are you now? What do you want to do next? What support do you need?'

We cannot make them feel or do anything. Ultimately, they choose what to do with the support you provide. However, if we think about our intention, we can influence how receptive they are to support and the choices they make.

Unsupportive dressed up as supportive

My client, Emily (not her real name), was an operations director who always strived to support her colleagues. When one of her team members, Mark (also not his real name), seemed overwhelmed with a challenging project, Emily immediately offered her assistance. She provided guidance, shared resources, and even offered to take on some of Mark's workload to alleviate the pressure.

However, despite Emily's best intentions, Mark became increasingly frustrated. He felt that Emily was taking over the project and undermining his abilities. In a tense conversation, Mark expressed his desire for autonomy and a chance to overcome the challenges alone.

While Emily was trying to demonstrate support, her actions were received as unsupportive. Realising her mistake, Emily apologised and acknowledged that she had disempowered him. She assured Mark that she believed in his capabilities and would provide support honouring his autonomy and professional growth. Emily shifted her approach by offering regular check-ins, a supportive listening ear and resources tailored to Mark's needs.

Through open communication and a more balanced approach, Emily regained Mark's trust and restored a positive working relationship. She learned that being professionally supportive requires understanding individual preferences, respecting autonomy and providing guidance that empowers rather than diminishes her team's confidence.

From that point forward, Emily adopted a more nuanced approach to support, recognising that each team member may require different levels and types of assistance. Her commitment to striking the right balance helped foster a supportive and productive work environment where colleagues could thrive while feeling empowered to overcome challenges on their own terms.

While Emily's intent was positive, this was a classic situation of unsupportive dressed up as supportive. Even with no malicious intent, the actions had unintended consequences for Mark and Emily.

To determine what unsupportive dressed as supportive can look like, here are some unsupportive and supportive phrases that are commonly used. You may find yourself using them more than you think.

Unsupportive phrases are quite directive and can lack empathy. Statements or questions that are unsupportive attempt to resolve rather than explore. This is often so when the person providing

Self-awareness guides
us to think about our
language and actions.
Through our connection,
we build trust and rapport.
In asking questions, we
open dialogue and seek
to understand rather
than tell what we know.

support shares a relevant experience connected to the issue at hand.

Supportive phrases create space as they use open rather than directive language.

Unsupportive phrases	Supportive phrases
You'll be fine.	How can I help you?
It could be worse.	Would you like to talk about it?
It reminds me of the time when....	I am here for you.
Seriously, put it into perspective.	I understand this must be difficult right now.
You just need to....	Can I call/contact someone for you?
Why is this still an issue?	Would you like to go for a walk?
I think you should....	Can I check in a little later today?

Ideal support looks different for different people. The most supportive thing we can do is to make it bespoke. Self-awareness guides us to think about our language and actions. Through our connection, we build trust and rapport. In asking questions, we open dialogue and seek to understand rather than tell what we know. In *calibrate*, we synthesise all available data points to determine their needs. In *support* we first ask, 'How can I best support you?' Then we act with the *intent* of helping them to feel confident, curious and courageous so they can explore, experiment and enact.

Reflection questions

How would my team members describe my current level of support? What specific areas might need improvement?

Can I identify instances where my actions or decisions may have inadvertently conveyed a lack of support? How could I have approached those situations differently?

What does 'being supportive' mean in my leadership role? How can I translate this into tangible actions for my team?

Am I attentive to the individual needs and aspirations of each team member? How can I tailor my support to better align with their goals?

Do I actively seek feedback from my team regarding the support I provide? How can I create an environment where they feel comfortable sharing their thoughts?

How can I empower my team to take ownership of their projects while offering guidance and encouragement?

CHAPTER 9

The Deliberate Leader Attributes

*'Before you are a leader, success
is all about growing yourself.
When you become a leader, success
is all about growing others.'*

– Jack Welch, former GE chairman and CEO

So far, we have explored self-awareness, trust, connection, asking the right questions, calibrating to make better decisions and offering optimal support. The reality is that not every leader can be a good coach. There are specific attributes they need to demonstrate.

We are talking about *leaders* as coaches, so we can't completely ignore the leader part. This may feel like unlearning what you know about leading and managing, and relearning based on some new and potentially familiar competencies or attributes.

What makes a great coach? In sports, some say the number of wins defines great coaching. I think it is more than that. Great coaching is about the success of the team beyond wins and coverage.

An Australian football league player commented that she could feel early in the season whether the team would be successful. She described the team dynamics team as critically important. She also talked about trust and openness and the attributes that create a successful team.

When a leader takes on coaching as a deliberate leadership style, their responsibility is to role model these attributes.

In the corporate world, we look to wins, translated as business success, targets met and goals achieved. We look at the culture of the team and the organisation. Does it feel good to belong to this team and this business? If we are successful, yet being in this team adversely affects me, I will assess the team's culture and the leader's role in condoning that culture.

Rather than focusing on the coach's effectiveness in driving the team to win, A.J. Becker suggests that a better way to measure coach greatness is to consider the experience of the athletes who play for them.[1] The experience links to how people are likely to feel and perform.

An athlete looks for connection with the team and the coach. Becker describes this as familiarisation with the coach, the coach-athlete relationship, the environment and the system. It's the same in the corporate world, where employees join an organisation seeking connection with their manager and team.

What makes a great coach? In sports, some say the number of wins defines great coaching. I think it is more than that. Great coaching is about the success of the team beyond wins and coverage.

(Hopefully, that connection has begun through the attraction and recruitment process.) They consider the environment, the culture and the systems and work out how things are done.

In a research study led by Becker, elite professional athletes were asked what makes a great coach.[2] They identified six key dimensions, including the characteristics and behaviours of the coach, the environment and system that the coach and coachees are in, relationships developed and coaching actions and the influence on the athletes concerning their performance and development. If we look closely, these dimensions have applicability in the corporate world. In this next section, we'll examine how these coaching attributes work for leaders who are coaches.

Coach attributes

The attributes of a great coach that positively impact athletes' experience on the team are:

▶ More than just a coach
▶ Personality characteristics
▶ Abilities
▶ Experience.

For example, being more than just a coach includes subthemes of a great person, teacher, mentor, friend, leader, expert and human being. These describe the roles of people we encounter who provide support and advice in various aspects of life. Traditionally, these characteristics are not areas a coach would delve into, as the coach's role is viewed as entirely separate from these roles. However, they highlight the typical positive characteristics that can be beneficial to the person being coached. These characteristics facilitate connection and may help to build trust in the coaching relationship.

We can separate the personality characteristics into four categories including:

▶ Cognitive
▶ Emotional
▶ Social
▶ Psychological.

We look at these characteristics through the lens of a leader who deliberately adopts a coaching style.

Cognitive

The same research reveals that a great coach is knowledgeable, smart, innovative and creative. They are revered for their expertise and ability to think strategically. They are more likely to be respected for their expertise and views (to the extent they share them). This has a positive impact on credibility, which helps to build trust.[3]

Being smart is not always about being 'book smart'. While cognition and acumen are essential in a coach, having a general level of 'smarts' (for example, being strategic, having intuition and being self-aware) also matters.

Being innovative was also recognised as a key attribute. A coach who can explore with you, encourage you to have a go and maybe

When we act 'as if',
we put ourselves in
an imaginary situation
and feel like we are
there. We can visualise
ourselves with zero
risk. This unlocks
creativity and enables
us to envision 'what if'.

even try something new helps you stretch out of your comfort zone and offers the elasticity to grow and stretch, encouraging new and evolved thinking.

Creativity is like being innovative, but I differentiate the two by incorporating more fun and play in creativity. To quote one of my mentors, Lisa, when we are creative, we act 'as if'. If I act as if I have already been promoted to the next level, what would I do, how would I act, and what would I say?

When we act 'as if', we put ourselves in an imaginary situation and feel like we are there. We can visualise ourselves with zero risk. This unlocks creativity and enables us to envision 'what if'. It's an important part of being a coach. To help someone connect with something they perceive as out of reach. Leaders can do this by asking questions, posing scenarios, and offering everyone's favourite — roleplay. (I think people like to dislike roleplays, but they are an effective experiential learning activity.)

Emotional

The themes identified for a great coach here are that they are passionate, enthusiastic, inspirational, calm but intense, and emotionally stable.

A passionate coach feels like they are all in. They are in your corner and care deeply about you. There is genuine kindness and care with an energy that is high, but not overbearing. They are connected to your goals and help you to achieve them. They are committed and dedicated, and demonstrate this through investing time and effort into you. They believe in your potential and work with your strengths to help you leverage these.

An enthusiastic leader offers positive energy and approaches their coaching role with optimism. They are eager to make a difference and driven by a strong desire to help others grow, succeed, and overcome challenges. They offer and encourage a growth mindset, which often looks like having an open mind and offering a different point of view.

It's hard to be inspirational, as it's very subjective. What is inspirational for one person may be inane or even offensive to another. An inspirational leader considers what motivates the person they are working with. It is less about the coach and more about the coachee. A great coach leverages motivation to inspire. If the person is uplifted by nature, perhaps the coaching conversation is relocated outside sometimes. The coach may recommend books or podcasts if the person is enlivened by learning. This is not necessarily about the coach being inspirational; it's more about evoking such feelings in others.

Calm but intense is an oxymoron. The words don't quite match, nor do 'friendly fight' or 'sweet sorrow'! A coach who is calm but intense offers steadiness with passion and intensity. They are focused but don't provoke anxiety or stress. It's amplified care. Their calmness provides reassurance and the intensity feels focused and present. They are there for you and you feel it, but aren't smothered by it.

Finally, in this category, we consider the value of an emotionally stable leader. These coaches are aware of their emotions, triggers and reactions and are mindful of how these factors influence their coaching interactions. This self-awareness allows them to manage their emotions effectively and respond to situations calmly and with composure. They demonstrate resilience and can assist coachees by sharing how to bounce back from difficult situations and setbacks without becoming overwhelmed or reactive. They maintain a positive outlook and find constructive solutions even in the face of adversity. They share this with others. Their ability to be empathetic, which we've covered extensively in this book, enables them to connect better and understand those they are coaching. They are also more likely to practise self-care than just talk about it. This helps them to be present and grounded.

Social

The coaching attributes in the social category are genuine, loyal, patient, honest, candid, flexible, non-judgmental, demanding, likeable, humourous, rare, special and balanced. Leaders who are sincere and authentic in their interactions, foster a deep sense of trust and connection. They genuinely care about their team's well-being and success. Loyalty is another important attribute, as coaches demonstrate unwavering support and commitment to their team, even during challenging times.

Patience is a valuable quality that gives the team the necessary space and time to explore their thoughts, emotions and goals at their own pace. Honest, candid coaches promote open and transparent communication, providing feedback and guidance with integrity. They cultivate a safe environment where coachees can be vulnerable and trust the coach's honesty.

Flexibility is essential in adapting leadership approaches and methods to meet each person's unique needs and preferences. Non-judgmental leaders create a safe and accepting space for the team to express themselves without fear of judgment. Demanding leaders set high expectations and challenge their coachees to reach their full potential.

Likeability and a sense of humour help foster a positive and enjoyable coaching experience. These attributes create rapport, ease tension, and encourage coachees to feel comfortable and open. Rare and special coaches possess unique qualities that make them stand out, offering a distinctive and valuable coaching experience.

Finally, balance is crucial for coaches to maintain their personal well-being while supporting others. They strive to find the equilibrium between empathy and objectivity, and care and professionalism. This balance ensures they provide optimal support and guidance while caring for their needs.

Psychological

Attributes identified under the psychological category include being confident, disciplined, competitive, perfectionist, dedicated, aggressive, meticulous, organised, committed, consistent and professional. While I don't agree with some of these attributes (namely perfectionist, aggressive and meticulous), it's worth exploring how others can translate into coaching behaviours.

Confident leaders believe strongly in their abilities and expertise, instilling confidence in the person they are coaching. Their self-assurance helps create a sense of trust and credibility. Disciplined coaches maintain a structured approach, setting clear goals and expectations for themselves and their teams. They demonstrate a strong work ethic and hold themselves accountable for their actions.

Competitive leaders embrace healthy competition, encouraging the team to strive for excellence and reach their full potential. They foster a mindset of growth and improvement, pushing the team to go beyond their comfort zones.

Dedicated leaders are fully committed to the team's success and well-being. They invest significant time and effort in understanding their coachee's needs and developing tailored strategies to help them achieve their goals. Organised coaches demonstrate strong planning and time management skills, ensuring smooth and efficient coaching sessions.

Committed leaders provide ongoing support and guidance, even in the face of challenges and setbacks. Consistency is a key attribute, as coaches maintain a steady and reliable approach, delivering their coaching with reliability and dependability.

Abilities and experience

The key abilities identified in the study of great coaches include adaptability, getting along with others, compartmentalisation, reading people, acting with integrity, and analysing and integrating professional and personal life.

When a leader is adaptable, they demonstrate that they are not stuck. That means they encourage stretching and rethinking views and can do this themselves. Adaptability does not mean that they don't hold firm views or are incapable of forming or holding a view. It means they are willing to adapt their view because they hold it lightly. Their views are thoughts to be shared rather than an extension of themselves or their identity.

Great leaders get along with others. They respect others' views even when they don't match their own. It's not about liking people or being likeable. It is about establishing positive and harmonious relationships through effective communication, empathy and mutual respect. It involves understanding and appreciating diverse perspectives, resolving conflicts peacefully, and fostering collaboration and cooperation.

Compartmentalisation is about understanding the big picture and the different components that make up the big picture while dealing with these separately and as required. A great coach may hear the problems a coachee poses and offer a perspective on choosing priorities to resolve them. That requires compartmentalisation to segment each component and sequence the order for attention and resolution.

The ability to read people is a super attribute for a coach. We looked at calibration earlier and understood how important it is for a coach to make sense of all the data points they receive from their coachee. Does it tell a part of a story? What questions are needed to help create and tell the rest of the story? Curiosity and questions help us to read people. Unless you have psychic ability, you must be inquisitive, join the dots and ask questions to reveal the missing information.

Great leaders get
along with others.
They respect others'
views even when
they don't match
their own. It's not
about liking people
or being likeable.

A deliberate leader can't be a hypocrite. They cannot coach without living the principles that guide their work. They have integrity. Their actions and words are consistent. Any inauthenticity may be tangible if there is incongruence between what they say to others and what they do. Your experience of them will be hollow — like the bottom of an ice cream cone. You want something to be there, but it's not, and you cannot help but feel disappointed.

Analysis is another vital attribute. They don't need to become stuck in the analysis, they just spend useful time there. Jumping to a conclusion can cost a leader and their team dearly. It can lead to a lack of understanding of the problem or challenge, and incorrect advice and guidance. Take time to understand by asking questions and expanding on the issues, providing time and space for analysis. Better diagnosis equals more effective treatment as a solution.

It takes a lot of energy to be someone different in your personal and professional lives. An authentic leader integrates these aspects and helps others to do the same. It's all about making things easier rather than distracting and tiring.

Any leader who chooses to coach may have a few extra and unique attributes, but the foundations are much the same.

The attributes of a Deliberate Leader

This next section explores the Deliberate Leader model. We'll look at eight core competencies, unpack what each competency is (and isn't), and the feedback you may receive if you don't demonstrate the competencies. That feedback is critical in understanding what you need to look out for when you are off track.

The attributes are identified through the persona of a deliberate leader who leads on purpose and with intention. One who embodies a unique blend of qualities and skills that enable them to guide, inspire and support individuals in their personal and professional growth. They possess a deep understanding of human psychology, a passion for helping others and a commitment to excellence.

As a reader of this book, you are likely looking to incorporate coaching strategies and techniques into your leadership practice. You may have attended formal coach training or be accredited in a coaching methodology. That may not matter to you, yet you still want to lead and incorporate coaching in your leadership. This section is about combining leading and coaching as a deliberate leader. Let's look at that in more detail.

First and foremost, they must be skilled communicators, actively listening, asking insightful questions, and providing constructive feedback. Effective communication creates a safe and non-judgmental space where their teams can freely express themselves and explore their thoughts and emotions.

As covered earlier, empathy is another essential trait. Coaches understand and relate to the experiences and challenges faced by their teams. Putting themselves in their shoes offers genuine support and guidance tailored to specific needs and circumstances. Familiarity with the team enables them to empathise at a higher level.

Ultimately, both coach and leader are catalysts for transformation. They empower individuals to experiment with their full potential, navigate obstacles, and create meaningful and fulfilling lives.

A strong sense of intuition and insight means they identify patterns, uncover underlying issues and help their team gain clarity and perspective. They facilitate self-discovery and personal growth by asking thought-provoking questions and guiding team members to find their own solutions. This reduces the burden of the leader needing to have all the answers all the time and increases accountability for team members to be resourceful and have a go.

As motivators and encouragers, they inspire their teams to set ambitious goals, push past their limits, and believe in their potential. They celebrate successes, no matter how small, and provide the necessary motivation and accountability to keep the team on track.

We know that integrity and professionalism are fundamental. Coaches adhere to ethical standards, maintain confidentiality and prioritise the best interests of their team. They are committed to ongoing professional development, continuously expanding their knowledge, and honing their coaching skills so they can offer the best they can to the team. They appreciate that learning is evolutionary.

Ultimately, both coach and leader are catalysts for transformation. They empower individuals to experiment with their full potential, navigate obstacles, and create meaningful and fulfilling lives. Their impact goes beyond the coaching relationship, leaving a legacy of growth, empowerment and positive change.

Replacing the word 'coach' with 'leader' fits perfectly. Why? The attributes of a great leader and a great coach are not dissimilar.

We are served equally well by leaders who choose to coach. If you choose to be a Deliberate Leader, you can coach.

Let's dive into the details of the Deliberate Leader attributes (Figure 8).

Figure 8: The Deliberate Leader model

Empathetic

What it is: A leader who understands and connects with the emotions and experiences of their team, providing a supportive and understanding environment.

What it isn't: A leader who tries to *feel* what someone else is feeling rather than *understand* what they may be feeling.

What it looks like:

▸ Understanding and sharing thoughts, feelings and experiences of others.

▶ Stepping into the shoes of their team members or colleagues and genuinely connecting with their perspectives and emotions.

▶ Demonstrating active listening skills, seeking to understand the needs, concerns and aspirations of those they work with.

▶ Creating a safe and supportive environment where individuals feel heard, valued and respected.

▶ Validating the emotions and challenges faced by their team.

▶ Demonstrating compassion and offering guidance without judgment.

▶ Attuning to non-verbal cues, recognising the unspoken messages and underlying feelings of others.

Indications you may need to work on being empathetic:

▶ Talking over others and interrupting them

▶ Dismissing others' comments or views

▶ Being unaware of others' emotions

▶ Making insensitive or hurtful remarks

▶ Being self-centred

▶ Communicating points of view in a blunt or insensitive way

▶ Confusing sympathy with empathy.

Encouraging

What it is: Enabling and motivating team members. Offering positive reinforcement and fostering belief in their capabilities.

What it isn't: A leader who criticises the team and uses guilt and shame to get the job done.

What it looks like:

- Inspiring, uplifting and supporting individuals towards their goals and aspirations.
- Providing positive reinforcement, fostering a growth mindset, and instilling confidence in their team members or those they coach.
- Recognising and acknowledging the efforts and achievements of individuals, and offering praise and appreciation for their progress.
- Providing constructive feedback in a way that motivates and empowers rather than demoralises.
- Creating an environment that nurtures continuous growth and development.
- Inspiring others to believe in their own potential, setting high expectations and providing the necessary support to help individuals stretch beyond their comfort zones.
- Fostering a positive and optimistic team culture where mistakes are seen as opportunities for learning and where challenges are viewed as stepping stones to success.
- Creating a sense of empowerment, resilience and enthusiasm within their teams. They inspire individuals to take risks, overcome obstacles and achieve their full potential.

Indications you may need to work on being more encouraging:

- ▶ Delivering feedback in a way that is harsh and lacks empathy
- ▶ Expecting others to be perfect all the time
- ▶ Creating a culture that does not tolerate mistakes and learning from setbacks
- ▶ Setting clear expectations and guidelines for individuals and the team
- ▶ Expecting accountability from team members
- ▶ Lack of variation in how you encourage and motivate team members.

Empowering

What it is: Coaches empower their teams to take ownership of their goals, decisions and actions, helping them develop confidence and self-reliance.

What it isn't: Restricting or diminishing an individual's autonomy, growth and decision-making ability.

What it looks like:

- ▶ Guiding and supporting team members while fostering a culture of autonomy, growth and self-belief.
- ▶ Providing individuals with the necessary tools, resources and opportunities to take ownership of their work and develop their skills.
- ▶ Encouraging collaboration and valuing the input and ideas of their team members.

▶ Actively involving individuals in decision-making processes, allowing them to contribute and have a sense of ownership over their work.

▶ Trusting in their team members' abilities and providing them with autonomy to make decisions and take on responsibilities.

▶ Investing in the development of team members, offering guidance, mentorship and growth opportunities.

▶ Providing constructive feedback, recognising achievements, and helping individuals identify areas for improvement.

▶ Supporting and challenging team members to reach their full potential while also ensuring a safe and supportive environment to learn from failures and embrace continuous learning.

Indications you may need to work on being more empowering:

▶ Taking away the opportunity for others in the team to make decisions

▶ Giving the individual a false sense of belief and ability

▶ Believing you know what they need without asking

▶ Sharing stories with the team to inspire and motivate

▶ Setting realistic goals within the team and supporting the team to achieve these

▶ Talking about having a growth mindset and what this means in the team or for the individual

▶ Being aware of actions that may diminish other team member's power.

Energetic

What it is: Coaches are intuitive, can sense the energy of the person they support, and understand what they need. They can adapt their energy so they can work with diverse energy types.

What it isn't: Turning up with inauthentic energy and not varying energy levels to suit the situation.

What it looks like:

- Bringing enthusiasm, vigour, and a positive attitude to their role.
- Natural energy inspires and motivates others, creating an environment of excitement, engagement, and high performance.
- Infusing interactions with enthusiasm and passion, creating a contagious energy that uplifts their team members.
- Approaching challenges with a can-do attitude and encouraging their team to do the same.
- Infectious energy helps drive momentum, innovation and a sense of purpose within the team.
- Realistic belief in team members' potential and the value of their work.
- Actively involved and present, bringing a sense of urgency and dedication to achieving shared goals.
- Overcoming obstacles, instilling resilience, and maintaining a positive outlook even in the face of adversity.

- ▶ Fostering a collaborative and supportive atmosphere, they encourage open communication, celebrate achievements, and provide timely and constructive feedback.

- ▶ Energy is a catalyst for teamwork, creating a cohesive and dynamic unit that thrives on collective success.

Indications you may need to work on being energetic:

- ▶ Not managing your energy as a leader

- ▶ Being insensitive to the energy of others

- ▶ Being unaware of the impact of your energy on others

- ▶ Expecting energy levels to be consistent (for you or the team) all the time

- ▶ Expecting high performance without factoring in rest and reflection time

- ▶ Being inauthentic about your levels of energy

- ▶ Encouraging the team to work on managing their energy.

Effective

What it is: Leaders who coach utilise proven methodologies and strategies to facilitate meaningful progress and positive change for their teams.

What it isn't: Having little regard for processes and organisation and leaving things to chance.

What it looks like:

- ▶ Communicating the bigger picture, including team purpose, goals and targets.
- ▶ Identifying and working with the team to create processes that support the work that needs to be done.
- ▶ Being adaptable and open to change.
- ▶ Taking an organised calm approach to getting the work done.
- ▶ Seeking other perspectives and considering them before acting or deciding.
- ▶ Expecting accountability to personal values for themselves and their team.
- ▶ Designing processes and procedures that enable the work to be done even when the leader is not present.

Indications you may need to work on being effective:

- ▶ Lack of processes and systems, leading to a feeling of disorganisation
- ▶ Clear and achievable goals haven't been identified or communicated
- ▶ Focusing on delegation so others can share accountability in goals
- ▶ Everything is consistently urgent
- ▶ Little time spent on planning the work
- ▶ Spending more time communicating and checking for understanding

▶ Sharing problems and issues sooner so others can assist.

Enthusiastic

What it is: Coaches bring a contagious enthusiasm and passion for their team's growth and development, igniting inspiration and drive.

What it isn't: Difficulty energising and building excitement in others.

What it looks like:

▶ Exploring opportunities in a positive way

▶ Having a growth mindset

▶ Ensuring that goals are easily understood

▶ Connecting teams to the goals and the work through engaging with them

▶ Inspiring others to connect to the vision and goals

▶ Seeing the best in self and others

▶ Focusing on leveraging and harnessing strengths.

Indications you may need to work on being more enthusiastic:

▶ Demonstrating excitement and dedication to goals and initiatives

▶ Utilising positive language

▶ Inspiring others in a way that works for them

▶ Motivating others for high performance and growth

- ▶ Sharing resources that may influence others to increase their feeling of enthusiasm
- ▶ Connecting others to the bigger goal
- ▶ Demonstrating care and being attentive to the team's needs.

Engaging

What it is: Coaches actively listen, ask probing questions, and fully engage with their teams, building trust and facilitating deep exploration.

What it isn't: Assuming that people are engaged just because they are in your team.

What it looks like:

- ▶ Showing interest in those you work with and the work that needs to be done
- ▶ Seeing team members are more productive because they feel energised, focused and aligned with their goals
- ▶ Focusing on connecting the team or the individual to the bigger picture
- ▶ Helping the team to understand how their contribution aligns with the goal
- ▶ Inviting input and sharing ownership
- ▶ Paying careful attention to the working environment so it can bring out the best in people
- ▶ Offering the opportunity for others to contribute before you do and asking lots of questions.

Indications you may need to work on being more engaging:

- ▶ Not thinking a lot about what motivates and engages others
- ▶ Believing that people should feel engaged if they have a job
- ▶ Caring more about the tasks rather than the people
- ▶ Being perceived at times as disinterested or preoccupied by others
- ▶ Not feeling engaged
- ▶ Lacking clarity about the purpose and vision of the organisation
- ▶ Unclear about your role as a conduit between those in your team and the organisation.

Explorative

What it is: Coaches actively explore through effective questions that expand thoughts and mindsets. This encourages new patterns of thinking and creates more expansive thinking.

What it isn't: Positioning yourself as the expert who knows stuff and doesn't need to explore.

What it looks like:

- ▶ Asking more questions than you answer
- ▶ Being comfortable with ambiguity
- ▶ Understanding that the answer that emerges through dialogue is likely to be of better quality

- ▶ Developing a growth mindset attitude for yourself and the team
- ▶ Properly defining the overarching issue to be solved
- ▶ Managing expectations of others so they understand the process of exploring and the outcomes to be achieved
- ▶ Exercising patience until the right answer emerges.

Indications you may need to work on being more explorative:

- ▶ Tending to shut down conversations rather than allowing exploratory dialogue
- ▶ Jumping to the answer, just to get on to the next issue
- ▶ Setting enough time to allow for deep exploration
- ▶ Appearing inconsiderate of the broader set of circumstances surrounding the issue
- ▶ Not managing time appropriately, so constantly being rushed
- ▶ Developing a deeper understanding of the broader issues and implications that may exist
- ▶ People relying on you for the answers.

These attributes enhance our ability to be deliberate leaders. We choose to lead all the time. The eight attributes work in harmony; ideally, you will be proficient in most of them. If not, consider how to lift your capability in those areas.

Leading like a coach requires specific competencies. Focusing on these competencies complements your leadership skills and enables you to have a great professional relationship with your team while achieving amazing things together.

Reflection questions

Rate yourself with a score out of ten for each Deliberate Leader attribute. How well do you demonstrate these attributes in your leadership?

Empathetic: __ /10

Encouraging: __ /10

Empowering: __ /10

Energetic: __ /10

Effective: __ /10

Enthusiastic: __ /10

Engaging: __ /10

Explorative: __ /10

Which are your highest rating attributes?

What are your focus areas for the Deliberate Leader attributes?

Why have you selected these as your focus areas?

What impact will focusing on these attributes have on your leadership?

What does your team need most from you?

CHAPTER 10

Developing a Deliberate Leadership Coaching Culture

'Culture is not an initiative. Culture is the enabler of all initiatives.'

— Larry Senn

Developing deliberate leaders who coach, benefits teams and organisational results. However, the higher impact is felt when we consider developing deliberate leadership coaching cultures. This chapter explores how organisations can benefit from doing so. We'll delve into the advantages, some key principles and practices, and the stages involved in creating and sustaining it.

Let's start with some case studies.

Think Talent

Ainsley Johnstone is CEO of Think Talent, a specialist recruitment agency based in Melbourne, Australia. As work dried up through the pandemic and forced disruption, Ainsley had space to reconsider the direction of the business and bring back an idea she'd had many years earlier. She wanted to elevate her team's performance and increase their sense of joy, happiness and engagement.

She thought about the tension she and the team had experienced. While a busy time meant intense periods of performance and stress, this did not result in high engagement. Individual targets, leading to lucrative rewards, didn't help either. So, Ainsley abolished this model and went to team incentives and rewards. Thanks to her dedicated team, performance was just as high, but stress levels were more manageable and engagement was higher.

The role of the chief talent activator is a new addition to the Think Talent team, but it's a role that Ainsley has had on her mind for many years. A fan of Gallup Strengths (Ainsley has hers proudly listed on her corporate bio), Ainsley wants to support her workforce by ensuring their unique talents are identified and leveraged. The chief talent activator works with the team to unlock performance gaps, help leverage strengths and, ultimately, drive high performance. This is complemented by a fair and egalitarian performance and reward structure that rewards team performance first and foremost.

This is a departure from most recruitment agencies and Think Talent's former reward structure that rewarded individual performance before team performance. When Ainsley spoke to her team about changing the goals and making them more team-based, they were far happier, more focused and more engaged. There was an increase in overall team performance and higher levels of engagement among the Think Talent team.

The introduction of the chief talent activator hasn't stopped Ainsley from coaching her team. It has freed her up to be a performer in the team, recruiting team members and supporting clients alongside her role as coach and CEO. She feels the team values this because her dual role of working on and in the business enables pace and growth with her team.

Time Etc

Time Etc was established in 2007 and provides virtual assistants to organisations globally.

As the business experienced fast growth with expansion in the US market, Time Etc started to experience some growing pains. Founder and CEO Barnaby Lashbrooke describes these as typical small business cultural issues. They were recruiting and found that some people would leave after six months, others found their job stressful and there were some toxic behaviours in the workplace.

A survey revealed that the team sought support in goal setting, feedback, personal and professional opportunities, and autonomy from their manager. Lashbrooke says the list sounded like they needed a coach more than a manager. They wanted someone in their corner — people who were prepared to give feedback, good or bad, elevate them, help them to do their best, listen to them, support them and help them grow.

That feedback brought Time Etc to where it is today. Lashbrooke attributes their switch to coaches rather than managers as key in why Time Etc consistently ranks in the top 1% of teams globally in the Gallup Q12 survey. The company has a culture of coaching instead of management, high levels of engagement and low levels of turnover. The organisation now has a ratio of one coach to six employees. The coach's mandate is simple: help employees be as productive as possible. These coaches still manage, but their focus is empowering and supporting employees to find their own way forward.

I asked Lashbrooke if coaching at Time Etc is more of a leadership style or philosophy. He believes it is authentic coaching. The coaches identify clearly as coaches rather than managers. Lashbrooke says this differentiation is a deliberate flag and point of difference in how they lead. Any pushback has been about a lack of discernment in selecting the right coaches. The essential qualities that Time Etc look for in their coaches are humility, determination, strong work ethic, grounded, understated, alignment with organisational values, and demonstrating a genuine desire to help others. The belief is that employees should be coached and not managed traditionally.[1]

Chevron

Chevron Corporation is an American multinational energy corporation predominantly involved in oil and gas. HR industry analyst Josh Bersin has closely followed Chevron's use of coaches in their learning and development offer. Since the program started in July 2020, more than 1,200 Chevron leaders have received personalised development, including coaching. More than 90% of these leaders say coaching makes them more effective at their jobs. In its Operational Excellence Management System, Chevron calls out that leaders are responsible for coaching, monitoring, and holding people accountable.[2]

Chevron has also implemented the use of coaching circles. In this initiative, Chevron leaders gather in small global groups to discuss and learn through expert-facilitated discussions. These programs have now reached more than 3,000 Chevron leaders in fifteen languages.[3] Chevron uses coaches as part of its leadership development suite of programs. As part of the Emerging Leader program, participants can select a coach who works with them to understand their leadership assessment and create a development plan. Chevron uses internal coaches that are certified in its programs.[4]

Bersin states that other benefits at Chevron from implementing coaching include a 15% increase in employee recognition, a 12% improvement in business alignment, a 13% improvement in problem-solving, and a 16% improvement in strategic planning. Coaching has helped the company transform its entire performance management process.

Beyond the best

As these examples show, there are huge advantages to developing leaders who coach, but we want to go beyond that. We aim to integrate coaching techniques as a way of being in organisations. The culture shifts when the entire organisation embraces coaching in all interactions, learning and growth. It moves from 'growth at all costs' to supported growth, and from unrelenting high performance to sustainable performance.

Teams feel less burnt out and more supported while developing themselves and achieving more. The coaching recipients experience noticeable growth, more confidence, focus and self-worth.[5] Developing a deliberate leadership coaching culture promotes a coaching mindset among leaders and becomes the practice of how we lead in organisations.

Significant challenges present great opportunities

The rate of change in organisations is ever-increasing. Our ability to respond to fast-changing consumer demands, technological advances, resource availability, and business strategy can feel like a washing machine on high spin.

Coaching can directly impact how an organisation performs and can be a strategic objective where the role of leaders is rapidly adapting and changing. Organisations need to be more nimble to survive in the changing business environment, where roles change regularly to meet increasing responsibilities.[6]

A leadership coaching culture fosters a supportive and empowering environment that enables employees to reach their full potential.

The rate of change in organisations is ever-increasing. Our ability to respond to fast-changing consumer demands, technological advances, resource availability, and business strategy can feel like a washing machine on high spin.

Defining a coaching culture

We have looked extensively at leaders who coach, now, let's turn to creating coaching cultures. Imagine an organisation that adopts coaching techniques and style throughout its entire operation.

A coaching culture refers to a work environment and mindset that values and promotes coaching as a critical approach to employee development, growth and performance improvement. It embraces the principles and practices of coaching throughout all levels of the organisation, from leaders and managers to individual contributors. As Clutterbuck and Megginson write, 'Coaching is the predominant style of managing and working together, and where a commitment to grow the organisation is embedded in a parallel commitment to grow the people in the organisation.'[7]

In a coaching culture, coaching is not limited to formal coaching sessions or interactions with external coaches. It becomes an integral part of the organisation's DNA, or ways of working, where the behaviours and techniques are ingrained in daily interactions, feedback, and leadership practices. It fosters a supportive and empowering environment where individuals are encouraged to take ownership of their development, learn from their experiences, and continuously grow their skills and capabilities.

The features of a coaching culture

Adopting a coaching culture requires deliberate intention and focus across the entire organisation. The organisations that have deliberately created and implemented them recognise it's a strategic move for stronger performance, engagement, and retention of key talent.

The role that leaders play in adopting a coaching culture is critical. Leaders always set the tone. Culture is created from the messages received about how people are expected to behave. Leaders set the boundaries for what is expected, tolerated and accepted. These boundaries come in the form of spoken and unspoken rules, behaviours, values and purpose.

Specific characteristics set it apart from other cultures. These include the way we learn, communicate, think, act and relate to each other. They are described in this next section.

Start with the fundamentals

The fundamentals establish the right foundation for the culture necessary for deliberate leadership.

A growth mindset: Carol Dweck, a leading authority on mindset, says that adopting a growth rather than a fixed mindset supports the notion that abilities can be developed.[8] Coaches with a growth mindset support others to evolve and seek feedback to improve.

Empowerment and accountability: The culture needs to support and encourage individuals to take ownership of their growth and development while holding them accountable for their actions and results.

Active listening and powerful questioning: A coaching culture focuses on time for deep listening and asking powerful questions to facilitate reflection, self-discovery and insights.

Feedback and constructive dialogue: Coaching cultures encourage regular feedback exchanges, creating opportunities for individuals to learn from both successes and areas for improvement.

Coaching skills for leaders: Coaching cultures prioritise development for leaders. This equips leaders and managers to develop their coaching skills to support team development, unlock potential, and foster a coaching mindset across the organisation.

Learning and development opportunities: Coaching cultures view learning and development as a constant, providing resources, training and support to help employees develop coaching skills and apply them in their roles. It is important to believe that abilities can develop and change and that coaching is an ideal way to facilitate this process.

A coaching culture enhances employee engagement and motivation, increasing productivity and satisfaction. Coaching supports individual and team performance improvement by unlocking potential, fostering learning, and providing guidance. It promotes talent development, boosts retention rates, and contributes to a positive organisational culture.

The model in Figure 9 illustrates the components of a deliberate coaching culture.

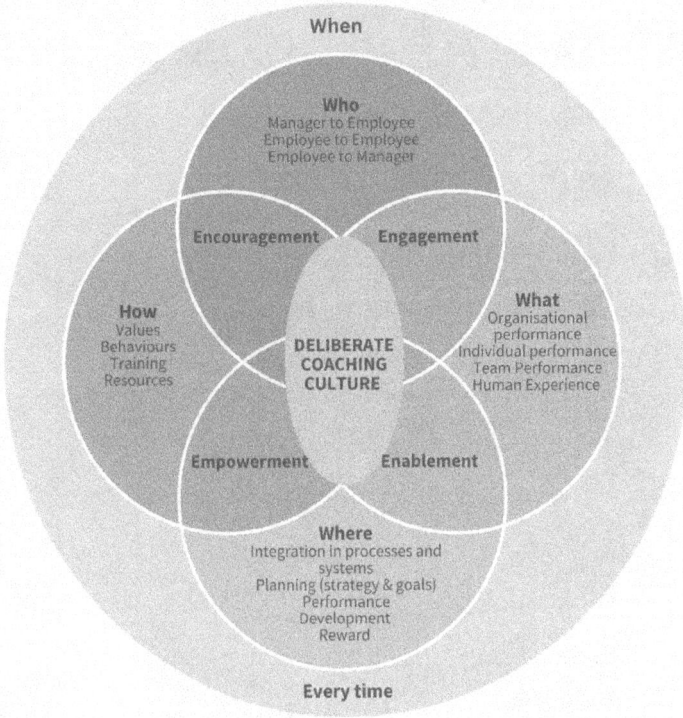

Figure 9: Deliberate coaching culture

A deliberate coaching culture

In Chapter Nine, we applied the elements of encouragement, engagement, enablement and empowerment to the coach as an individual. These are equally necessary and valid in an organisation. Coaching need not be limited to didactic interactions in teams. It can have a significant positive impact and apply in all areas of the operations of a business.

Let's look at how to implement a deliberate coaching culture. There are five key questions to consider:

A successful
organisation with
a strong positive
culture consistently
monitors results
and pays attention
to actions, beliefs
and experiences.

1. When do we need a deliberate coaching culture?
2. How do we instil it?
3. Who does it impact?
4. What does it impact?
5. Where does it show up in organisations?

When do we need a deliberate coaching culture?

When do we focus on implementing and utilising a deliberate coaching culture? All the time. Every time. It cannot be an initiative that has phases or comes and goes. Consistency is the key to embedding a coaching culture.

Research by organisational culture consultants, culture.io, supports that culture is based on results, actions, beliefs and experiences.[9] Organisational culture represents visible symbols and behaviours, demonstrated values and deeply embedded assumptions that contribute to an organisation's unique social and psychological environment.[10]

A successful organisation with a strong positive culture consistently monitors results and pays attention to actions, beliefs and experiences. When initiatives supporting the implementation of coaching cultures are integrated with other business initiatives, leader support is strengthened and there is continued investment towards sustaining the environment.[11]

How do we instil a deliberate coaching culture?

Culture is expressed in how we do things in an organisation. We see it demonstrated, positively and negatively, through the values and behaviours of those in the organisation. In creating a coaching culture, the values and behaviours must support what is intended to be achieved through the culture.

A deliberate coaching culture has values like empowerment, inclusiveness, ownership, collaboration, innovation, accountability and learning.[12] Alongside these, the organisation may define actions that enact the values. To have a strong coaching culture, an organisation needs to be clear on its values and behaviours, and know that everyone consistently observes and applies them.

Those values and behaviours can be supported with resources such as training workshops, development programs and guides. Training ensures that people understand the values and know how to apply them through demonstrated behaviours. An organisation may articulate what the values and behaviours look like — and what they don't look like.

Who does a deliberate coaching culture impact?

In an organisation, coaching is often thought of as a one-to-one relationship: one coach and one team member. However, in a coaching culture, all organisation members can coach. Coaching is no longer specialised; it can be delivered by a range of individuals in different capacities.[13] Coaching moments can happen anywhere, at any time. Employees coach when they have self-awareness and trust, and when they connect, ask, calibrate and support each other through questions and feedback. The coaching relationship could be manager to employee, employee to employee or even employee to manager. Levels and hierarchy are less relevant because we are all learning and can learn from anyone at any time.

What does a deliberate coaching culture impact?

Companies implementing a coaching culture have found that it benefits the business greatly by promoting more open communication, greater trust and respect, and improved working relationships.[14] It can positively impact organisational performance, individual performance, team performance and the human experience.

When the decision is made to pursue a coaching culture, it is about more than coaching programs and training. A deliberate cultural transformation infuses the benefits of coaching across every level of the organisation. These benefits are felt through all interactions, processes and systems.

Where do organisations have a deliberate coaching culture?

You won't just see a coaching culture in one-to-one conversations between a coach and an employee; there's evidence throughout the organisation. We see encouragement, engagement, empowerment and enablement in processes and systems, planning (strategy and goals), performance, development and reward.

While coaching has typically been used as a strategy to develop leaders or as part of a suite of leadership development initiatives, integrating coaching with other development and talent management processes is critical to achieving the full benefit.[15]

The mindsets of a coaching culture

In addition to the five key questions explored above, four mindsets enable a coaching culture. They are encouragement, engagement, empowerment and enablement.

Encouragement

Encouragement is essential because it fosters a positive and supportive environment for growth and development. When encouraged, individuals feel acknowledged and motivated to push beyond their limits, resulting in increased confidence and resilience. Encouragement helps individuals embrace challenges, learn from failures, and strive for continuous improvement. It builds trust and rapport between coaches and coachees, creating a safe space for open communication and feedback. By emphasising encouragement, a coaching culture cultivates a mindset of optimism, empowerment and collaboration, enabling individuals to reach their full potential and achieve meaningful outcomes.

Engagement

Engagement fuels active participation and commitment from leaders and teams. When engaged, individuals are fully present and invested in the coaching process, which enhances learning and development. It fosters open dialogue, promotes self-reflection, and encourages exploration of new ideas and perspectives. Engagement creates a sense of ownership and accountability, motivating individuals to set and pursue meaningful goals. By prioritising engagement, a coaching culture ensures that individuals feel heard, valued and supported, leading to increased collaboration, creativity and, ultimately, transformative growth.

Empowerment

Empowerment promotes autonomy, confidence and ownership of one's actions and decisions. By empowering individuals, a coaching culture cultivates a sense of self-belief and capability, allowing them to take charge of their development. It encourages them to set ambitious goals, take risks and explore their full potential. Empowerment also nurtures a growth mindset, enabling individuals to embrace challenges, learn from setbacks, and adapt to change. By fostering a culture of empowerment, coaches create an environment where individuals are inspired to become their best selves, leading to increased innovation, resilience, and personal fulfilment.

Enablement

Enablement is central to a coaching culture because it focuses on equipping individuals with the necessary tools, resources and skills to succeed. By enabling individuals, a coaching culture ensures they have the support and guidance to overcome obstacles and achieve their goals. Enablement promotes continuous learning and development, providing opportunities for skill enhancement and knowledge acquisition. It fosters a culture of collaboration and teamwork, where individuals are encouraged to share their expertise and support each other's growth. By prioritising enablement, coaches create an environment that empowers individuals to thrive, driving performance, productivity and personal fulfilment.

Benefits of a deliberate coaching culture

A coaching culture offers numerous benefits to organisations. Most importantly, it improves performance through a structured process focusing on clear goals, objectives and outcomes.[16] This enhances employee engagement and motivation. Empowering employees through coaching conversations means they feel valued, heard and supported in their professional development. Engaged employees are more committed, productive and satisfied, leading to higher levels of performance and retention. Coaching supports individual and team performance improvement by unlocking potential, fostering learning, and providing guidance. A coaching culture promotes talent development, boosts retention rates, and contributes to a positive

By enabling individuals, a coaching culture ensures they have the support and guidance to overcome obstacles and achieve their goals.

organisational culture. It also enhances employee engagement and motivation, and improves individual and team performance.

Building blocks of a deliberate coaching culture

In his book *Trust and Inspire*, Stephen M. R. Covey shares that culture is a significant determinant in attracting, retaining, engaging and inspiring the best people to work in your organisation.[17] Organisations focus on culture, as it is often the primary differentiator between organisations. Multiple organisations can produce and sell the same thing. They may even be in the same city, with similar equipment and similar buyers. What differentiates these organisations is their culture, how they do the work and what behaviours are demonstrated. What shared goals, beliefs, routines, needs or values are in place.[18]

When considering a coaching culture, key factors are manager commitment, a link between strategy and developmental focus, recognition and reward of coaching behaviours, training for coaches, and learning and development opportunities.[19] Organisations that successfully embed a coaching culture ensure support for coaching across the entire organisation, vertically and horizontally. This willingness should come from all levels, from coach to coachee. To develop a coaching culture, organisations must establish several foundational elements:

- Leadership commitment and role modelling
- Integration of coaching skills into leadership development programs
- Aligning coaching with organisational goals and values

▶ Creating a safe and supportive environment for coaching.[20]

Leadership commitment and role modelling

Developing a coaching culture starts at the top. Senior leaders must endorse coaching as a valuable approach and model coaching behaviours. When leaders prioritise coaching, it sends a clear message to the rest of the organisation. As we learned from Think Talent's story, the CEO recognised the importance of incorporating coaching practices to support her team.

While some organisations engage external coaches, introducing internal coaches (like the chief talent activator role at Think Talent) has several benefits. Where direct managers play a coaching role, there is a more rapid building of trust and respect for the person, their role and their goals.[21]

Implementing a coaching culture can be thwarted if leaders don't embrace the use of coaching skills or do not actively support it throughout their organisation. They are integrated into the organisational culture and have a more profound knowledge of the business strategy and goals. When a consistent coaching practice is developed and used across the organisation, it becomes an established part of the organisational culture.

In a survey about the key components of a coaching culture, 75.4% of managers cited consistency in different types of coaching across the organisation as central to developing a coaching culture. They cited senior leadership support, training and resources as the essential elements, alongside alignment with organisational values, transparency of benefits, and established and communicated processes about coaching.[22]

Integrating coaching skills into leadership development programs

Coaching skills should be incorporated into leadership development programs to equip leaders with the necessary competencies. Training programs must focus on active listening, powerful questioning, providing constructive feedback, and fostering a growth mindset. When a coaching culture is embedded, coaching is simply how we lead and learn. At Time Etc, this was a key strategy in developing a coaching culture.

This applies to how leaders lead, develop, motivate and reward, and how all employees (including leaders) learn, including how we listen, give and receive feedback, teach, train, influence, perform and grow. Formal acknowledgement of developing expertise in coaching can be reflected in coach training for leaders and peer-to-peer coaching for employees.

Alignment with organisational goals and values

A coaching culture supports aligning and attaining organisational goals, and drives higher performance. Turner says a coaching culture is supported by a 'multi-level leadership strategy supported by systematic, results-focused performance management, aligned HR processes and relationship-driven leadership coaching behaviours designed to achieve an engaged, committed workforce and a high-performance culture'.[23] Coaching initiatives should align with the organisation's mission, vision and values. Leaders and employees see the direct connection between coaching and organisational success by linking coaching to strategic objectives.

Creating a safe and supportive environment for coaching

Creating a safe and non-judgmental space where coaching is encouraged fosters trust and openness. Organisations establish a culture that values learning, growth and feedback. Leaders create psychological safety, allowing employees to take risks and share openly without fear of repercussions.

Developing deliberate coaching skills in leaders

Leaders play a crucial role in shaping a coaching culture. Leaders who use a coaching style enhance their leadership abilities. Tomkins says that when a manager takes on a coaching role, there is more collaboration, delegation, listening, a greater level of questions, and more specific feedback.[24] Organisations looking to develop managers as coaches can improve coaching skills among leaders by focusing on these key areas.

- ▶ Identifying coaching competencies
- ▶ Offering coach training and development
- ▶ Providing ongoing support and supervision
- ▶ Applying coaching practices in day-to-day interactions.

Training should
include theoretical
knowledge and
hands-on practice
to build confidence
and competence.

Identifying coaching competencies

Organisations define the specific coaching skills and behaviours that leaders should possess. These competencies may include active listening, empathy, effective questioning, providing feedback, and fostering employee growth.

Offering coaching training and development

Comprehensive coaching training programs provide leaders with practical tools and techniques. In a 2023 survey of HR professionals, 85% reported that coaching skills are critical for leaders to develop in the next three years.[25] Training should include theoretical knowledge and hands-on practice to build confidence and competence. In a study of coaching in organisations, 38.8% of 580 Australian managers described appropriate training and resources as a fundamental component of a coaching culture.[26] Without a formalised approach, there are inconsistencies in applying and adopting a coaching culture, impacting its ultimate sustainability. Time and investment are essential to have the fullest impact on an organisation.

Providing ongoing support and supervision

Continuous support through training, coaching supervision, mentoring, or peer coaching must be embedded to complement the initial training, for leaders to continue to develop their coaching skills. That allows leaders to reflect on their coaching practices, seek guidance and continuously improve their skills. Using accountability partners or leaders who coach networks could also provide ongoing support.

Applying coaching practices in day-to-day interactions

Encouraging leaders to practice coaching skills regularly and integrate them into their leadership approach means that coaching development initiatives are deliberate. A coaching culture is present in every interaction. Leaders should incorporate coaching conversations into their interactions with team members, using coaching techniques to support growth, address challenges, and foster development. Organisations can support integrating a coaching culture by identifying coaching competencies for leaders, providing training and development opportunities, offering ongoing coaching support and supervision, and encouraging leaders to practice coaching in their daily interactions.

The DDI Global Leadership Forecast 2023 reported that companies focusing on coaching for development see major benefits, such as clearer development paths, a greater sense of accountability for being an effective leader, and greater retention, with employees choosing to stay in their organisations to advance their careers.[27]

Embedding deliberate coaching practices

A consistent approach to embedding coaching practices into the organisational culture sustains the benefits of a coaching culture. It should be embedded in:

▶ Coaching conversations and feedback

- ▶ Goal setting and performance management
- ▶ Career development and succession planning
- ▶ Team coaching and collaboration.

Coaching conversations and feedback

An organisation can change the focus from one-on-ones to coaching conversations that support growth and development. Regular feedback exchanges become an opportunity for coaching and learning. Leaders should focus on active listening, asking powerful questions, and providing constructive feedback that helps employees identify areas for improvement and growth.

Goal setting and performance management

Integrating coaching principles into goal-setting processes and performance management systems helps to embed a coaching culture. Instead of solely focusing on performance evaluation, leaders engage in coaching conversations that help employees set challenging but achievable goals, identify strategies for improvement, and provide ongoing support. This does not diminish performance as a priority but enhances it by focusing on skills and strengths.

Career development and succession planning

Supporting employees' career aspirations through coaching conversations, identifying development opportunities and providing guidance on career progression can help employees gain clarity on their career paths, identify their strengths, and develop strategies to enhance their skills and competencies. This strengthens career development and succession planning benefits for the individual and the organisation. At Chevron, the use of coaching circles and incorporating coach training in leadership development played a significant part in developing their culture.

Team coaching and collaboration

Coaching is not limited to one-to-one interactions between a leader and an employee. Through the promotion of coaching within teams to enhance collaboration, communication, and problem-solving skills, team members support each other's growth, share knowledge and best practices, and work together to achieve shared goals. This peer-to-peer coaching can occur with or without the leader present, which promotes accountability for maintaining a coaching culture across the entire team.

Overcoming challenges and resistance

When introducing a coaching culture, organisations may face challenges and resistance. Time, cost, perception of effectiveness, and the need for trained coaches can all present barriers. There is a misperception that adopting a coaching culture is labour-intensive, expensive, and difficult to assess, but the implementation is no different from any organisational change. A change process must be deliberately planned and followed to mitigate any risk of negative impact.

Leadership expert John Kotter suggests an eight-step process for leading change in organisations.[28] This process could equally be applied to implementing a coaching culture, which would maximise the chances of a successful implementation and integration. I have built on Kotter's eight steps below, connecting them to implementing a coaching culture.

1. **Establish a sense of urgency.** Why does this coaching culture need to be implemented now? What does it seek to address that is a pressing issue for the organisation?

2. **Forming a powerful guiding coalition.** Are the senior executive team on board? If not, why not? What will it take for them to agree to adopt and support the implementation of a coaching culture?

3. **Creating a vision.** What will the implementation of a coaching culture look like for the organisation? What is the vision for what is to be achieved through a coaching culture?

4. **Communicating the vision.** Don't keep this a secret. Let others know the intended benefits and what they will do for the organisation.

5. **Empowering others to act on the vision.** What will get in the way of achieving this vision? What systems or processes need to be changed or reviewed? Does the vision feel like it belongs to everyone in the organisation?

6. **Planning and creating short-term wins.** What will success look like as we implement a coaching culture? Where are we expecting to see short-term benefits?

7. **Consolidating improvements and producing more change.** What systems, processes and structures need to be reviewed or changed to fit our vision of a coaching culture? Have we embedded the fundamental principles

of our coaching culture in all that we do across our organisation?

8. **Institutionalising new approaches.** Have we updated, aligned and embedded values and behaviours that support our coaching culture? What else do we need to review and make changes that reflect our coaching culture?

Resistance is likely when you embark on any significant culture change. It's important to address these challenges proactively. Some strategies to strengthen the success of the implementation could include:

Addressing concerns: Proactively communicate the value and benefits of coaching culture to alleviate scepticism or resistance. Address common concerns and misconceptions, emphasising the positive impact coaching can have on individuals and the organisation.

Demonstrating impact: Share success stories and examples of how coaching has positively influenced individual and organisational performance. Highlight tangible outcomes, such as improved employee engagement, enhanced performance, and increased retention rates. These examples can serve as compelling evidence of the value of coaching culture.

Training and support: Offer ongoing training, support and resources to help leaders navigate challenges and build confidence in their coaching abilities. Provide opportunities for leaders to share experiences, learn from each other, and seek guidance from experienced coaches or mentors.

Continuous evaluation and improvement: Regularly assess the impact of coaching initiatives and make adjustments based on feedback and data. Collect feedback from leaders, employees and other stakeholders to evaluate the effectiveness of coaching practices, and identify areas for improvement.

Sustaining a deliberate coaching culture

Like most things, implementation is the start; it's not where we finish. The next focus needs to be on sustaining it. To ensure longevity, consider how to reinforce it by recognising and celebrating milestones, ensuring the coaching culture is incorporated into all processes and ensuring its impact can be measured.

Here are some tips on sustaining a coaching culture in your organisation.

Continuous reinforcement: Provide regular reminders, resources and opportunities for leaders to continue developing their coaching skills. That might include refresher training sessions, coaching circles, or communities of practice where leaders can share experiences and learn from each other.

Recognising and celebrating coaching successes: Acknowledge and celebrate leaders who demonstrate exceptional coaching practices. Recognition can motivate others to embrace coaching and contribute to a positive coaching culture.

Incorporating coaching into all talent management processes: Integrate coaching principles into all talent management practices, such as performance reviews, succession planning, and leadership development programs. By aligning coaching with existing processes, organisations reinforce the importance of coaching as a core leadership competency.

Measuring the impact on organisational outcomes

Establish metrics and measurements to assess the impact of coaching culture on key performance indicators such as employee engagement, productivity, retention rates, and organisational success. Regularly evaluate the progress and impact of coaching initiatives to ensure ongoing improvement.

The impact on organisational success

The impact of a deliberate coaching culture on organisational success is well-researched and documented. It should not be considered a remedy for a problem; rather, it's a way to achieve a higher performance culture. We benefit from healthier cultures and improved business results.

A 2015 study across 498 Spanish firms confirmed that coaching influences individual and organisational performance indicators.[29] The hypothesis tested was that improvements in individual performance as a result of coaching positively affects firm performance and growth. The study proved that coaching processes benefit individuals, which leads to organisational benefits, such as sales increases and productivity growth, producing a unique value proposition.

In another study of a Fortune 500 company, coaching was linked to a 529% return on investment. Of the respondents, 77% indicated that coaching significantly impacted at least one of nine business measures, and 60% could link specific financial benefits to their coaching.[30]

A survey of 5,700 HR specialists found benefits for coaching recipients and their organisations. Coaching generated improvements in recipients' performance targets and goals by 84%. It increased openness to personal learning and development by 60% and increased the identification of solutions to specific work-related issues by 58%. For organisations, it increased the utilisation of individual talents by 79%. Organisational performance and productivity increased by 69%.[31]

Organisations implementing coaching skills notice improved employee performance and empowerment and employees feeling valued, increasing the likelihood of staying with their organisations.[32]

The examples of Think Talent, Time Etc and Chevron show that coaching success can be measured using tangible metrics, including organisational performance, growth, productivity, employee engagement, culture and retention. When the impact of coaching is objectively measured, it reduces the risk of the initiative not being supported. It supports the continuance of coaching as a leadership style that significantly impacts all levels of the organisation.

This chapter has looked at a macro view of incorporating coaching into leadership. We have moved beyond the relationship between the leader and the team, and into the entire organisation. When coaching is accepted and incorporated across the organisation, culture and performance experience positive shifts, enhancing the experience of everyone in the business.

Reflection questions

How does the concept of a deliberate leadership coaching culture align with my organisation's current values and goals?

What potential barriers or resistance might arise when introducing a deliberate leadership coaching culture, and how can they be addressed?

As leaders, what specific steps can we take to model and promote coaching behaviours within the organisation?

How can we ensure that coaching becomes an integral part of daily interactions rather than an isolated initiative?

What metrics or indicators could we use to measure the success of a deliberate coaching culture?

How can continuous learning and improvement be embedded in our deliberate coaching culture over time?

Afterword

Developing and implementing a leadership coaching culture is a transformative journey for organisations. By fostering a coaching mindset among leaders, organisations can empower their employees, enhance engagement, and drive higher performance. Leadership commitment, skills development, and embedding practices create a supportive environment where coaching becomes integral to the organisational culture. The benefits of a coaching culture are far-reaching, leading to improved growth, engagement, and performance within organisations. Embracing coaching as a leadership approach can transform organisations and unlock their full potential.

Leading like a coach takes self-awareness. You must be able to observe the impact of your behaviours and ways of working, and adjust and modify them as required.

Leading like a coach requires building and maintaining trust — the foundation of any relationship. When you coach someone, trust needs to be reciprocal and deep. There is also an understanding that trust needs to continue to be a focal point. Just because it is there now, doesn't mean it will be there forever.

The Deliberate Leader model involves connecting, asking, calibrating and supporting. These modes are underpinned by self-awareness and trust.

A coach connects with their people to establish rapport, credibility and trust. This helps drive positive outcomes for the individual and the organisation.

A coach asks, because assumptions are shortsighted and focus on knowing rather than seeking to understand.

A coach calibrates to synthesise all available data points before making a decision, sharing an opinion or asking a question.

A coach supports by not presuming to know what support an individual requires but by asking how they can best be supported.

A leader who coaches benefits when they are aware of and can demonstrate these essential attributes. These strengthen relationships, deepen trust, increase self-awareness and create a high-performing culture.

Developing a coaching culture creates real and measurable business benefits. When coaching is so ingrained that it is infused in the culture of an organisation, everything is done through a coaching lens, benefitting the individual, the team and the organisation.

In a coaching culture, an organisation offers encouragement, empowerment and enablement and can better engage all stakeholders. This is felt at all levels of the organisation and impacts what is done and how it is done.

Implementing a coaching culture is no less significant than embarking on cultural change. It must be planned with a clear vision, executive endorsement and support, consultation, and a robust change management process.

The business benefits of having leaders who coach and implement a coaching culture are tangible and measurable. They positively impact growth, productivity, achievement of results, engagement and retention.

We are in an era of quiet and loud quitting, volatility in market conditions, a shortage of talent across many resources, sectors and countries, and rapid technological change — all of which have the potential to change the world as we know it. Deliberate leaders reduce the impact of these threats, improve our workplaces and create environments where people enjoy working.

Are you ready to be a Deliberate Leader?

About the Author

Rita Cincotta works with leaders to elevate their impact so they can create engaged teams, successful organisations and connected communities. Her clients describe her as innovative and pragmatic. Her family tells her she is nurturing and impatient. Rita describes herself as an eternal optimist, curious about different perspectives.

What got Rita here? A whole lot of varied life experiences. And a few other things...

She has led HR teams and held C-suite roles in human resources in various industries, including technology, health, financial services and higher education. Rita is a highly experienced executive coach, having worked with leaders at all levels across most sectors. She is the author of *Evolve: The Business Partnering Playbook* and now *You Are How You Lead*. Rita is also a director on the board of a public hospital.

Rita works with organisations to help them develop a culture that delivers an optimal experience for their teams and customers. She facilitates programs on team and individual performance, leadership development and trust, and speaks at conferences.

The Deliberate Leader and Lead Like a Coach programs

For more information about the Deliberate Leader and the Lead Like a Coach programs, go to

www.ritacincotta.com

Implement a coaching culture in your organisation

If you are keen to discuss how you can implement a coaching culture in your organisation, reach out directly to Rita

rita@ritacincotta.com

Join our Leadership Impact Community

Join our Leadership Impact Community and receive resources, data and insights, and access to masterclasses and workshops.

https://ritacincotta.com/elevate-your-leadership-impact/

Acknowledgements

My sincere thanks to the clients who have invited me into their organisations to deliver the Leader as Coach program over the past five years. Working with you has taught me so much about what it takes to be a great coach in a professional setting.

To my coaching clients, thank you for trusting me to be your coach. It is always an honour and a privilege to be allowed into your world, to understand the intricacies of your challenges, fears, opportunities and wins. The exchange of energy is special. I treasure it and am forever grateful.

Thank you to my team Alana, Charlene, Jenefer, Karen and Chris. We run fast and have fun doing it. I am truly grateful for your support, dedication and belief in me. You allow me to practice what I preach in leadership and coaching. Having a great team is vital in any business, and I am grateful for you all.

To my mentors, Jane, Colin, Col, Lisa and Matt, the way you have all supported me over the last three years has enabled me to achieve what was a hope and a dream to start with. Your wisdom is always front of mind and guides many decisions. Thank you for inspiring, encouraging and energising me to practice my thought leadership and do what I love every day.

To my accountability buddies Maria and Sam, I am so grateful for your friendship and counsel. Thanks for your continued support over the years. I love that we cheer each other on from our different corners of the world.

To Jenny, the book would simply not be here without you. Your expertise in editing, publishing, exploring ideas gently and with huge impact, your gentle nudges and steers and your patience are what every author needs. I thank you, and it has been a pleasure to work with you again.

To Sylvie and the team at BookPOD thank you for making this book come to life. Your professionalism is outstanding, and I have loved working with you on this book.

To my extended family, my Mum, my beloved late Dad, Eva, Julius, David, Lana, Michael, Cindi, Orlando, Amy, Bianca, Genevieve and Madison, you all keep my feet firmly planted on the ground and remind me how lucky I am to have such a wonderful family. I am grateful for you all.

And to my home team, Darren, Matthew, Siena and Noah. Thank you for your patience and understanding and for cheering me on as I wrote this book. Thank you for your love and support. Thank you for enabling me to do what I do every day. I love you.

References

Chapter 1: The Deliberate Leader

1. Feldman, D. C. & Lankau, M. J. (2005) Executive Coaching: A Review and Agenda for Future Research. *Journal of Management.* https://doi.org/10.1177/0149206305279599

2. Bozer, G. & Jones, R. J. (2018) Understanding the factors that determine workplace coaching effectiveness: A systematic literature review. *European Journal of Work and Organisational Psychology*, 27(3), 342–361.

3. Kampa-Kokesch, S. & Anderson, M. Z. (2001) Executive Coaching: A Comprehensive Review of the Literature. *Consulting Psychology Journal: Practice and Research*, 53, 205-228.

4. Colomo, R. & Casado, C. (2006, August) Mentoring and Coaching. IT Perspective. *Journal of Technology Management and Innovation.*

5. Boyatzis, R. E., Smith, M. & Van Oosten, E. (2019, September-October) Coaching for Change. *HBR Magazine.*

6. Ted Lasso, Apple + TV 2020-2023.

7. George, B. & Clayton, Z. (2022, October 06) Successful Leaders Are Great Coaches. *Harvard Business Review.*

8. https://blog.gitnux.com/business-coaching-industry-statistics/

9. Fyfe, M. (2022, January 29) 'You're awesome and you're doing great': Why life coaches are in demand. *Sydney Morning Herald.*

10. https://coachingfederation.org/

11. Tompkins, M. W. (2018) Coaching in the Workplace. *Journal of Practical Consulting*, Vol 6 Iss 1, Pg 115-122

12. Newton, P. & Bristoll, H. (2013) *Principles of Coaching.* Free Management Books.

13. Wiles, J. (2023, May 01) Survey Signals Pause-and-Pivot Year for CEOs. *Gartner.* https://www.gartner.com/en/articles/survey-signals-pause-and-pivot-year-for-ceos

14. Cincotta, R. (2023) Collection of leadership challenges. The Leadership Lane Program.

15. Cheruvelil, K. S., Soranno, P. A., Weathers, K. C., Hanson, P. C., Goring, S. J., Filstrup, C. T. & Read, E. K. (2014) Creating and maintaining high-performing collaborative research teams: The importance of diversity and interpersonal skills. *Frontiers in Ecology and the Environment, 12*(1), 31-38. https://doi.org/10.1890/130001

16. Blanchard, K. & Hersey, P. (1969) *Management of Organisational Behaviour.* Prentice Hall.

Chapter 3: The Importance of Self-Awareness in Coaching

1. Hari, J. (2022) *Stolen Focus.* Bloomsbury Publishing Ltd.

2. Ashley, G. & Reiter-Palmon, R. (2012) Self-Awareness and the Evolution of Leaders: The need for a better measure of self-awareness. *Journal of Behavioural and Applied Management.* https://doi.org/10.21818/001c.17902

3. Bluckert, P. (2005) The foundations of a psychological approach to executive coaching. *Industrial and Commercial Training, 37*(4), 171–178. https://doi.org/10.1108/00197850510602060

4. Laske, O. (1999) An integrated model of developmental coaching. *Consulting Psychology Journal: Practice and Research, 51*(3), 139–159.

5. Sliding Doors (1998) Intermedia Films.

6. Salovey, P. & Mayer, J. D. (1990) Emotional Intelligence. *Imagination, Cognition and Personality, 9*(3), 185–211.

7. Quinn, R. E., Fessell, D. P. & Porges, S. W. (2021, Jan 15) How to Keep Your Cool in High-Stress Situations. *Harvard Business Review.*

8. Ashley, G. & Reiter-Palmon, R. (2012) Self-Awareness and the Evolution of Leaders: The need for a better measure of self-awareness. *Journal of Behavioural and Applied Management.*

9. Eurich, T. (2019, May 31) Why Self-Awareness Isn't Doing More to Help Women's Careers. *Harvard Business Review.*

10. Church, A. H. (1997) Managerial Self-Awareness in High-Performing. *Journal of Applied Psychology*, 281-292.

11. Lesser, E. (2004) *Broken Open.* Random House Australia.

12. Luft, J. (1969) *Of Human Interaction: The Johari Model.* Mayfield Publishing Co.

Chapter 4: Earning the Trust to Coach

1. Mayer, R. C., Davis, J. H. & Schoorman, F. D. (1995) An integrative model of organisational trust. *Academy of Management Review*, 20, 709– 734.

2. Zak, P. (2017, Jan-Feb) The Neuroscience of Trust. *Harvard Business Review.*

3. Zak, P. (2017) *The Trust Factor: The science of creating high performing companies.* AMACOM.

4. Endelman Trust Barometer (2022) *Special Report - Trust in the Workplace.*

5. Covey, S. M. R. (2022) *Trust and Inspire: How truly great leaders unleash greatness in others.* Simon & Schuster UK Ltd.

6. Zak, P. (2017, Jan-Feb) The Neuroscience of Trust. *Harvard Business Review.*

7. Lencioni, P. (2002) *The Five Dysfunctions of a Team.* Jossey Bass.

8. Duhigg, C. (2016, February 28) What Google Learned From Its Quest to Build the Perfect Team. *New York Times*, https://www.nytimes.com/2016/02/28/magazine/what-google-learned-from-its-quest-to-build-the-perfect-team.html

9. Edmondson, A. & Mogelof, J. P. (2005) Explaining psychological safety in innovation teams: Organisational culture, team dynamics, or personality? *Creativity and Innovation in Organisational Teams.* 109-136. 10.4324/9781410615732.

10. Core Strengths, Building Trust In A Coaching Relationship. https://www.corestrengths.com/building-trust-coaching-relationship

11. Development Dimensions Data (2023) Global Leadership Forecast.

12. Frei, F. & Morriss, A. (2020, May-June) Begin with Trust. *Harvard Business Review*.

13. Trusted Advisor and Associates. *Understanding the Trust Equation*. https://trustedadvisor.com/why-trust-matters/understanding-trust/understanding-the-trust-equation

Chapter 5: Connect to Lead

1. Fairfield, M. (2015) Human Connection: Uncharted Territory for Value Creation. *Journal of Creating Value*, 1(2), 159–173. https://doi.org/10.1177/2394964315569629

2. Maslow, A. H. (1943) A Theory of Human Motivation. *Psychological Review*, 50(4), 370-96.

3. McLeod, S. A. (2007) Maslow's Hierarchy of Needs. http://www.simplypsychology.org/maslow.html

4. Ben-Hador, B. (2023) The practice of manager as coach (MAC): Unequal power relations and their effect on feelings toward the organisation. *Human Resource Development Quarterly*, 1– 22. https://doi.org/10.1002/hrdq.21497

5. Gaskell, C. (2007) Measuring the Impact of Coaching. *Personnel Today*, 26-27. https://www.proquest.com/trade-journals/measuring-impact-coaching/docview/229869365/se-2

6. Bregman, P. (2020, April) Empathy Starts with Curiosity. *Harvard Business Review*.

7. Hodges, S. D. & Klein, K. J. K. (2001) Regulating the costs of empathy: the price of being human. *Journal of Socio-Economics*, 30:437–452.

8. Hougaard, R. & Carter, J. (2022) *Compassionate Leadership: How to do hard things in a human way*. Harvard Business Review Press.

9. Hougaard, R., Carter, J. & Afton, M. (2021) Connect with Empathy, But Lead with Compassion. *Harvard Business Review*.

Chapter 6: Asking the Best Questions

1. Whitmore, Sir John & Performance Consultants International (2017) *Coaching for Performance, The principles and practice of coaching and leadership.* Nicholas Brealey Publishing.

2. Kofman, F. (2006) *Conscious Business.* Sounds True.

3. Boysen, S. M., Arya, T. & Page, L. (2021) Organisational and executive coaching: Creating a coaching culture in a non-profit. *International Journal of Evidence Based Coaching and Mentoring,* Vol 19 (2) pp 115-132.

4. Wiseman, L. (2017) *Multipliers, How the Best Leaders Make Everyone Smarter.* Harper Business.

Chapter 7: Calibrate to Lead

1. Oxford Dictionary online.

2. O'Connor, J. & Lages, A. (2004) *Coaching with NLP.* Element Publishing.

3. Grinder, R. & Bandler, J. (1987) *Reframing.* Real People Press.

4. Beattie, G. (2016) *Rethinking Body Language: How hand movements reveal hidden thoughts.* Routledge.

Chapter 9: The Deliberate Leader Attributes

1. Beattie, G. (2016) *Rethinking Body Language: How hand movements reveal hidden thoughts.* Routledge.

2. ibid

3. Maister, D. H., Galford, R. & Green, C. (2001) *The Trusted Advisor.* Simon & Schuster.

Chapter 10: Developing a Deliberate Leadership Coaching Culture

1. Lashbrooke, B. (2023, June 5) A company replaced all of its managers with coaches. Employees became 20% more productive—and much happier, *Fortune Magazine.* https://

fortune.com/2023/06/05/company-replaced-managers-coaches-employee-productivity-much-happier-work-careers/

2. Chevron, *Operational Excellence Management System*. https://www.chevron.com/-/media/shared-media/documents/OEMS_Overview.pdf

3. Bersin, J. (2021) *The Explosive Growth in Coaching: One of the Biggest Trends in Business.* https://joshbersin.com/2021/10/the-explosive-growth-in-coaching-one-of-the-biggest-trends-in-business/

4. Ellis, R. K. (2022) Building Chevron's Leadership Pipeline. *Association for Talent Development.* https://www.td.org/atd-blog/building-chevrons-leadership-pipeline

5. Tompkins, M. W. (2018) Coaching in the Workplace. *Journal of Practical Consulting*, Vol 6, Iss 1, Pg 115-122.

6. Rhodes, J., Lok, P., Yu-Yuan Hunh, R. & Fang, S. (2008) An integrative model of organisational learning and social capital on effective knowledge transfer and perceived organisational performance. *Journal of Workplace Learning*, 20 (4), 245-258.

7. Clutterbuck, D. & Megginson, D. (2005) *Making Coaching Work: Creating a coaching culture.* Charted Institute of Personnel and Development.

8. Dweck, C. S. (2006) *Mindset: The new psychology of success.* Random House.

9. Culture Partners. *Uncovering Key Factors That Determine Culture Strength.* www.culture.io

10. Schein, E. C. (2010) *Organisational Culture and Leadership.* New York; John Wiley and Sons.

11. Anderson, M. C. (2005) *Bottom-Line Organisational Development.* Boston MA; Butterworth-Heinemann.

12. Milner, J., Milner, T. & McCarthy, G. (2020) A coaching culture definition: An industry based perspective from managers as coaches. *The Journal of Applied Behavioural Science*, 56 (237-254).

13. International Coach Federation and Human Capital Institute (2014) *Building a Coaching Culture.*

14. Eldridge, F. & Dembkowski, S. (2004) Creating a Coaching Culture: 10 success factors for bringing it to life. *The Coaching and Mentoring Network.*

15. Anderson, M. C., Frankovelgia, C. & Hernez-Broome, G. (2016, February) *Creating Coaching Cultures: What Business Leaders Expect and Strategies to Get There.* Center for Creative Leadership.

16. Rolfe, J. (2010) Change is a Constant Requiring a Coach. *Library Management*, 31 (4/5). 291-303).

17. Covey, S. M. R. (2022) *Trust and Inspire.* Simon & Schuster UK Ltd.

18. Taylor, C. (2005) *Walking the Talk, Building a culture for success.* Random House Business Books.

19. Mansor, N. N. A., Syafiqah, A. R., Mohamed, A. & Idris, N. (2012) Determinates of coaching culture development: A case study. *Procedia-Social Behavioural Sciences*, 40, 485-489. https://doi.org/10.1016/j.sbspro.2012.03.220.

20. Milner, J., Milner, T. & McCarthy, G. (2020) A Coaching Culture Definition: An Industry-Based Perspective From Managers as Coaches. *The Journal of Applied Behavioural Science 56*:2, 237-254.

21. Newton, P. & Bristoll, H. (2013) *Principles of Coaching.* Free Management Books.

22. Milner, J., Milner, T. & McCarthy, G. (2020) A Coaching Culture Definition: An Industry-Based Perspective From Managers as Coaches. *The Journal of Applied Behavioural Science 56*:2, 237-254.

23. Turner, P. (2010) *Aligning Organisational Coaching with Leadership Behaviour.* (Published doctoral dissertation) Birmingham City University.

24. Tomkins, M. W. (2018) Coaching in the Workplace. *Journal of Practical Consulting*, Vol 6, Iss 1 Summer 2018.

25. DDI Global Leadership Forecast 2023. *Build Leaders Coaching Skills.*

26. Milner, J., Milner, T. & McCarthy, G. (2020) A Coaching Culture Definition: An Industry-Based Perspective From Managers as Coaches. *The Journal of Applied Behavioural Science 56*:2, 237-254.

27. DDI Global Leadership Forecast 2023. *Coaching Cultures are Effective but Dwindling.*

28. Kotter, J. P. (2007) Leading Change: Why Transformation Efforts Fail. *Harvard Business Review Magazine.*

29. Nunez-Cadro Utrilla, P., Grande, F.A. & Lorenzo. D. (2015) The Effects of Coaching in Employees and Organisational Performance: The Spanish Case. *Intangible Capital*, Vol 11 num 2, pp 166-189.

30. Wilson, C. (2004) Coaching and Training in the Workplace. *Industrial and Commercial Training*, 36 (3), 96-98.

31. Newton, P. & Bristoll, H. (2013) Principles of Coaching. Free Management Books.

32. Tompkins, M. W. (2018) Coaching in the Workplace. *Journal of Practical Consulting*, Vol 6 Iss 1, Pg 115-122.